Dr. John Demartini, a polymath and world-renowned human behavior expert

"Darren Jacklin's newest book, Until I Become, *is a thought-provoking masterpiece that will inspire, empower and catalyze ever greater levels of meaningful achievement."*

Mitzi Perdue (Mrs. Frank Perdue), Founder, Win This Fight, Stop Human Trafficking Now

"You can transcend your limitations... and let Darren Jacklin be your guide. Reading this book will enable you to create your own shortcut to success."

Jason Gesing, CEO, eXp Realty; Director, eXp World Holdings, Inc.

"Darren's story has inspired many audiences around the world for years. Until I Become *is sure to move and enlighten all those who've not yet had the good fortune to be among them."*

UNTIL I BECOME

Purpose, PERSEVERANCE, Payoff

DARREN JACKLIN

Until I Become: Purpose, PERSEVERANCE, Payoff

Published by Clovercroft Publishing, Franklin, Tennessee

Published in association with Larry Carpenter of Christian Book Services, LLC
www.christianbookservices.com

Project Management and Creative Direction by Tatiana Mersiadis

Cover design by Results Faster

Interior design by Adept Content Solutions

Printed in the United States of America

978-1-954437-23-4

The highest reward for a person's toil is not what they get for it, but what they become by it.

—John Ruskin

ACKNOWLEDGMENTS

This book is dedicated to the over one million people who have attended my live, in-person Global Corporate Training Seminars and especially to those who drove through snow storms, those who flew domestically and internationally to attend, and those who were required to attend because of work obligations then unexpectedly ended up falling in love with training and development.

This book is dedicated to my Dream Team: Jenette Longoria, the whole team at Tony Jeary International Team including Melina Adashefski, Daniel Marold, and Ella Imrie who collectively invested thousands of hours from early mornings to late nights, including weekends.

Everyone, at some point in their life, has a dream or a vision of who they could be. As we grow, sometimes that vision gets battered, minimized, or even obscured.

This book is dedicated to that vision of who you are meant to be. That is the real you. It has always been there. Having a glimpse of that vision is like a lick of ice cream, and as Buckminster Fuller said, "You wouldn't be given a lick of the ice cream unless you were meant to have the whole cone!" So I'll say it again: This book is dedicated to you. The *real* you.

And finally, this book is dedicated with the greatest love and admiration to my queen Tatiana. If it wasn't for your equal dedication to working on this book with me, it would not have been written.

CONTENTS

Candid photo of Darren with eXp's CEO, Jason Gesing—always looking for ways to add value

The freedom of being location independent is bound to make you smile

Thumbs up with the legend Tommy Hopkins—it's always great to team up with like-minded people, so be intentional about your tribe

Meeting Michael Gerber, author of *The E-myth*—one of the best books in the world

FOREWORD

Darren came into my life a few years ago and immediately impressed me with his thirst to both meet and connect people. As we got to know each other, more and more mutual connections began to surface, and our relationship grew faster. I became fascinated with his ability to follow through, which was demonstrated by his persistence in helping to connect me with other interesting, successful people who might benefit from my supercharging strengths. Our organization, Tony Jeary International—High Performance Resources, helps winners win more. Darren is a special colleague and friend. He's not only a winner, he also personally knows tons of winners, and he too helps and advises winners. It was only natural that we would connect professionally and even become buds.

From time to time, Darren and I would meet over the years on occasion at my RESULTS Center in Dallas.

We would brainstorm and discuss our respective goals. I've also had the pleasure of working with his talented team members during several of these meetings. I've also had the distinct pleasure of working directly with Tatiana, Darren's thought-provoking COO and life partner, during our team collaborations. A while into our coaching, I discovered that Tatiana had not only read a few of my books; they were actually sitting behind her on a shelf during our calls. I began to realize that Darren and his team were committed to learning and growing, often through books, so I proposed my publishing company to launch his first book. As we unpacked the initial idea, it became clear that Darren absolutely

needed to share his life experiences, wisdom, research, and principles with the rest of the world.

After careful deliberation, we all agreed on a vision for this book. We're proud to bring you a compilation of fascinating stories from Darren's life that are all carefully centered around the theme of *Perseverance*. The book is divided into bite-size messages that will inspire you just like Darren does when you're listening to one of his world-class presentations or even when you're simply near him. Get ready for a journey! This transparent and truly open book has the potential to expand minds, promote self-reflection, and make both you and your organization better! Let's go.

—Tony Jeary, The RESULTS Guy™

INTRODUCTION

There was a time in my early twenties when I was living off welfare and selling watermelons on the side of the road. One day, I struck up a conversation with a very wealthy, successful real estate investor who had been purchasing my watermelons in bulk. He had the academic education of a third grader, believing that life was a far greater teacher than formal school. Our lives couldn't have been more different, yet we quickly became friends. He started taking me for rides around the city in his old Lincoln Town Car. The car reminded me of a big boat, with comfortable seating that made you feel like you were sitting in a cozy living room.

During one of our cruises, he stopped and pointed out a vacant lot. He pulled over. "Get out of the car. What do you see?" he demanded in his deep, gruff voice. Shaking nervously, I explained that all I could see was an empty piece of land, overgrown with weeds and surrounded by a rusty chain link fence. "You've got to change your thinking! You're going to stay broke thinking that way!" he shouted, while pounding on the hood of the car. "When you change the way you *look* at things, the things you look at change." We approached the lot and paused, taking it in. He excitedly shared his vision with me, saying, "I see a booming three-story commercial real estate complex here. I see opportunity zones. It's about learning to turn a crisis into an opportunity." I later realized that this man was teaching me about mindset. This experience marked the beginning of my journey from being an employee, who trades time for money, to an entrepreneur, who sees possibilities in everyday life.

For the longest time, I thought opportunities only came to a select few individuals. I thought people needed certain qualifications—such as an MBA, PhD, luck, or generational wealth—in order for the universe to bless them with glory and gold. Opportunities had surrounded me my entire life, yet I was blind to them simply because my mindset was broken. The biggest thing holding me back, though, was my lack of adequate understanding needed to see the problem. I didn't know my beliefs were self-limiting. I couldn't envision a reality beyond the one I was living. I was on the streets selling watermelons because, up until that point, I had been stepping over and walking past one opportunity after another. Just as my mind perceived a desolate lot full of weeds, my ego had fooled me into thinking that my identity was that of a fruit salesman and nothing more.

People often struggle to see themselves in a new position or career because their egos don't like risk. A major shift in identity often leaves people feeling very vulnerable. "What are people going to think about me? Am I going to be rejected? If I leave this company and start over at

"When you change the way you *look* at things, the things you look at change."

a new one, are my colleagues going to treat me differently?" The thing is, life is all about making choices, seizing opportunities, and every now and again, taking a leap of faith. My life immediately improved when I started letting go of my fears and self-limiting beliefs and began embracing calculated risks. The success story that lies in the pages ahead can be traced back to the simple yet powerful lesson that one of the most important guiding principles in life is limiting our exposure to potential liabilities and managing risk.

Are you the type of person who sees potential opportunity? Do you go through life riding the fence, or are you willing to make the jump? My goal is to give you as much perspective, wisdom, and understanding as I possibly can so that you'll be better equipped to overcome challenges much like my own. I've chosen to organize the content of this book according to the nine values that matter most to me personally. My experience has taught me that if you have an unrelenting focus and dedication to your values, then it becomes easier to manifest a life that brings you joy, pride, and fulfillment. Our hierarchy of values define who we are. They affect how we interact with the rest of the world, and they influence our decisions—both consciously and subconsciously. Each chapter includes lessons from my life that explain what it means to accept, and live by, that particular value. If you haven't already done so, take a moment to list out your own set of values. As you make your way through my list and related stories, I encourage you to reflect on your own life. Consider moments when your actions aligned with your list of values and perhaps also when they didn't.

I've shared much of my story with millions of people over the years, but this book is a little different. Most people get uncomfortable at the thought of divulging personal secrets—especially when this means admitting errors—but it's pointless to hold on to this discomfort. By letting go of shame and embarrassment, I've allowed myself to explore

Life is all about making choices, seizing opportunities, and every now and again, taking a leap of faith.

and learn from many of my biggest mistakes. More importantly, this process has positioned me so that I may share these lessons with you! *Until I Become* is an opportunity for me to shed light, give back, and express my number-one love language—acts of service.

Past pain and suffering are things that few people speak of openly. The condition of being human—in a physical body on this earth—means that no person can fully escape trauma. Whether big or small, everyone experiences trauma, and unless you work through it, you will unknowingly bring it forward to your present and future life. This book is a way for me to continue on my journey toward healing by studying my values more deeply than ever before. Above all, though, it's about you. This book was compiled with community in mind, which is why the first chapter is "Service"—the value at the very top of my list.

I am moved, touched, and inspired at the chance to help others in this new way. For many years now, the focus of my career has been on helping others uncover blind spots in their world. The same passion for serving people that has fueled my career and personal success is responsible for this work. My hope is to bring you insights that may prevent you from making the same mistakes I did, or at least to the extent that I did. If you're struggling to find your footing in life, if you're content with your life, or even if you're doing quite well, I'm confident my story will help you. I'll also periodically share books that have influenced me in different ways and at different points throughout my life. You'll notice I've included a *Very Important Points, or VIPs,* section at the end of each chapter to help drive home meaningful ideas and concepts. These sections are also a great way to quickly find and highlight main points.

VIPs

✔ The secret to living is giving. Enrich your life by putting the needs of others before your own. (Chapter 1)

✔ Having the mindset of an innovator can help you recognize opportunities to solve countless problems, which can in turn translate to a bigger bank account. (Chapter 2)

✔ Seek mentors, training, and development opportunities to help you discover your blind spots. (Chapter 3)

✔ Learn to embrace the present moment and celebrate the simple things in life. (Chapter 4)

✔ If you want real relationships that enrich your life, you must be real with others and especially with yourself. (Chapter 5)

✔ It's tough to be transparent with others when you are not in tune with yourself. The more you understand yourself, the better you're able to help other people understand themselves and the world around them. (Chapter 6)

✔ When you have the right mindset, collaboration becomes a powerful problem-solving tool. (Chapter 7)

✔ Tenacity is fundamental to every success story—past, present, and future. (Chapter 8)

This is an opportunity for you to gain a more complete vision of the future you've always dreamed of—the life that reflects your own design and an abundance mindset. I believe knowledge is one of the greatest gifts we can give each other. So rather than interpreting my message as a hard-and-fast lesson, think of it more like a gift from me to you—you're free to accept, decline, or counteroffer! Most of all, I encourage you to make the very best of it.

Regardless of which continent you call home, we all have the same need for love and connection

eXp ringing the closing bell at NASDAQ for the first time in 2018

"Humanitarian trips were something I've always dreamed of doing"- Darren

Enjoying teamwork with the founder of eXp World Holdings Glenn Sanford as well as Gary DiGrazia Sr., Gary J DiGrazia, and Derrick Ruiz

A LETTER TO
MY YOUNGER SELF

Dear Darren,

If I could go back in time and spend even just an hour with you, there are so many things I'd like to say. For starters I'll let you in on a little secret—all those grown-ups around you are just people that are still growing up too. You parents, teachers, counselors, and even grandparents don't know everything there is to know! Don't ever think that just because someone is older, they have all the right answers—especially not the right answers for *you*. Some of them are going to struggle fitting you into certain boxes that they've built. These boxes are supposed to help most kids, but they don't always help everyone. They're going to say that you're not like the other kids, they're going to separate you from the rest of them, and unfortunately these things will make you feel very lonely. People are going to say the things that make you different and special will forever prevent you from living a good life, but you're going to prove them all wrong.

You are gifted in ways that most people can't see, which means your childhood will be tougher than most other kids'. Darren, you're going to have to work hard, but you can and will do hard things! Your parents are going to do their best to help you; however, they're going to experience problems of their own. This is going to make things more challenging for you. Even if it seems like their love for each other has changed, remember that their love for you has not. I know this may be difficult to imagine right now, but when you're a little older, you're not going to love yourself much anymore. You're going to be unkind to yourself, and I wish so badly that I could stop you from hurting yourself emotionally or physically. When you think things couldn't possibly get any worse, they will. When you think you've hit rock bottom, you will fall even further. But I promise you that your pain is temporary and will not last forever.

I can't tell you exactly why things happen the way they do; however, I can say that one day, when you're older, you're going to experience immense gratitude for all that you have overcome. You will transform, create, and give back in more ways than you can imagine. Your life is likely going to surprise you in amazing ways as well. All those moments when you felt sad, alone, lost, afraid, ashamed, and powerless will eventually make more sense to you one day, and, in a weird way, you'll actually be grateful that they happened. Until then, I want you to know that I am your biggest fan in the entire world. I believe in you, I love you, and I can't wait for you to do the same. And remember, just because you're different does not mean you're broken.

CHAPTER 1
SERVICE

Service to others is the rent you pay to be here on earth.

—Muhammad Ali

My experience has taught me that the secret to living is *giving*. The adversities I faced throughout childhood and adolescence set me back in many ways, and I've had to overcome a difficult learning process with regards to being of service to others. After deciding to turn my life around, my instinct was to focus entirely on myself, and I took an entry-level position making cold calls. Day after day my duties involved making over 400 daily calls; little did I know that I was getting paid to learn a skill that would serve me for the rest of my life. Despite being rejected over one hundred thousand times throughout a five-year period, I pushed on. This translates to a rejection rate of over ninety percent. The other ten percent expressed interest, but this did not mean that the deal was closed. There is no doubt I had the mindset of a go-getter, but self-interest was always at the forefront of my mind. This created a new set of problems. My motivation levels were at a record high, and yet I wasn't seeing the results I was working toward. One rejection after another, I began to sense there was something seriously wrong with my approach to business. After about three months of spinning my wheels, I found myself behind in paying my phone bill once again.

I made a conscious effort to get honest feedback from customers, and I quickly discovered that my priorities were out of order. By focusing on myself and my own benefit, I was failing to build relationships with potential clients and customers. They could sense I was putting my needs before their own, which is why I kept struggling to close. Although I didn't know it at the time, I was coming from lack and scarcity. I had a mindset of desperation, rather than one of abundance and prosperity. For years, people had convinced me that my learning disabilities would make it nearly impossible to read or retain information. This message was repeated to me so many times that it became an ingrained part of my self-image. It wasn't until I was introduced to Dale Carnegie training in 1994 and Toastmasters in 1995 that I was in a position to challenge these beliefs. I was positive that the only way I could learn was through massive action and experience, so I began reading, networking, and being in conversation with a lot of people about the art of giving. It was time to refocus my energies.

What are some of the opinions you hold toward yourself that are not accurate and are holding you back?

The chains that I had dragged along for so many years finally began to loosen. With a shift in attitude away from myself, knowledge and understanding started flooding in. My own behavior started surprising me. Rather than focusing solely on self-promotion, I brainstormed different ways that I could simultaneously champion others. I thought about my local community and began asking small business owners such as hairdressers, massage therapists, and reflexologists for small gift certificates and discount coupons. After explaining how this would bring customers through business development and create a win for everyone involved, they were more than happy to grant my request. I'd bring a few of them with me wherever I went, looking for opportunities to surprise people with a certificate tucked inside a handwritten thank-you card. I sought out people in different environments such as fast-food restaurants and grocery stores who displayed exceptional service. These little gestures not only sparked conversations about me, which generated business opportunities, but they also supported hard-working members of our community who typically received less recognition than they deserved.

A friend named Leslie often supplied me with discount coupons and gift certificates for haircuts at her salon, Miracles Hair Design. One day a woman approached me and pulled me aside to thank me for one of these coupons. As a single mother, she had been postponing getting her hair cut because she had to choose between paying for her children's school supplies for the upcoming year and getting her hair done. She couldn't afford to do both. With a job interview approaching, she really wanted to put her best look forward. Thanks to the gift certificate, she no longer had to choose. To top it all off, she ended up having a life-clarifying conversation with the stylist! Needless to say, I felt like a hero and honestly more successful than ever before.

When you strategically champion and support others in your community or network, everyone wins.

By actively choosing to make service a top priority in my life, I've created nonlinear opportunities that appear in unusal or unforseen patterns and opened new doors for myself—often completely unintentionally. When new introductions are made, our first impressions are usually lasting ones. The reality is that we are either memorable or entirely forgettable. As someone who has been on both sides of the coin, I can honestly say that serving others has personally made me more memorable. Knocking on doors at the ripe age of seven taught me the importance of making a good impression. More importantly though, it taught me that when you go above and beyond the call of service, people will remember you. Every now and again someone will be so moved, touched, and inspired by interacting with you that they'll want to share their experience with others. This is how I was able to promote myself at such a young age. It's also precisely how I've been able to build my success in life.

The subject of service brings back countless lasting memories that continue to inspire and remind me never to lose sight of what serving others can bring to one's life. Several years ago, I led an on-site corporate training and team-building seminar for an insurance company. Our team filled a fifteen-passenger van, and when lunchtime rolled around, we accidentally ended up ordering way too much food. After a little brainstorming, we decided to load up the team along with the leftovers and drive down to the inner-city Watts District in Los Angeles. Most of us had never previously interacted with people from the inner-city areas. We were all out of our element; however, food is a great icebreaker. It wasn't long before obvious tension turned into hugging and joy. This was in no way part of the corporate training program, and yet I was thrilled that our entire team had been part of this experience. For many, this was a first. It taught us all that some of the best acts of service can be entirely spontaneous.

If you are ever in excess, consider those who are in need.

Tony Robbins' book *Notes from a Friend* really influenced my understanding of what it means to be a giver. Tony tells a story about a stranger who came to his house with an offering of food. At the time, his father was too proud to accept the gift, so he turned the man away even though his family was in need. This moment made Tony realize that even complete strangers *do* care enough to be of service to others. He was so inspired by this experience that he created an entire philanthropic organization called the Anthony Robbins Foundation in the early 1990s. Shortly after, the foundation began hosting an annual US Thanksgiving Basket Brigade to feed families in need by providing them with baskets of donated food and household items. To this day Tony's foundation and charity event continue to remind us that you don't have to personally know someone in order to show you care.

When I returned *Notes from a Friend* back to my local library, I made a personal promise to myself that I would do whatever it took to spend time with Tony Robbins. I believed strongly in surrounding myself with successful people who have proven results. I didn't have enough money to pay for his courses, so I got creative. The Canadian Anthony Robbins Foundation took me on as a volunteer coordinator, and over the next five years I contributed over 2000 hours of my time. In exchange, I was able to attend Tony's Mastery University to learn from the man himself. Witnessing firsthand Tony's commitment to serving was eye-opening. It made me realize that I was capable of helping even more people by teaching others about the importance of service. Influenced by Tony's example, I went on to replicate this same idea in Vernon, British Columbia, Canada, on behalf of the Anthony Robbins Foundation.

The movie *Pay It Forward* inspired me and broadened my understanding of what it means to be a "go-giver." The first time I saw it was in my twenties on a tiny television set when it was released on VHS.

In the film, a young middle schooler starts a movement to change the world for the better. He brings life to the theory that when good deeds are paid forward, a ripple effect sweeps through the world touching countless lives with positivity. This movie made me realize that kindness often begets kindness. The effects of one small, seemingly insignificant

act of kindness often stretches farther than we think. It's the little things that make a big difference. *The Peaceful Warrior* is another powerful film that embodies acts of service. During one scene, the main character criticizes his mentor for choosing to work at a gas station. The mentor responds by explaining that he chooses to pump gas because the job allows him to serve others and that there is no higher purpose. I was so moved by the scene that I decided to rent out an entire theatre in Kelowna, British Columbia, and invite over 200 people to pass along this powerful message of service. This experience taught me that being of service to others can simply mean sharing ideas that transform the human spirit.

While sharing an office with Town & Country Tree Service, I reached a position where it became clear to me that there was an opportunity to really serve and make a difference in people's lives. Energized by this possibility, I made a point to write a special quote on the whiteboard in my office every day so that each visitor would be positively influenced. One of my favorite quotes was, "If you're good, I'll make you better. If you're better, I'll make you the best." I love this message because if you truly own it, you have the potential to help someone become a better father, mother, employee, business owner, or a better citizen in society.

I've been fortunate enough to cross paths with many people who have set a high standard for putting others first. These people came from all walks of life and socioeconomic backgrounds, yet they were all successful in their own ways too. Many years ago, a woman named Debbie Peebles started working for a Canadian hotel in the housekeeping department. Over the next twenty-five years she worked in nearly every department and proved herself worthy of several major promotions. Eventually, she earned the title of General Manager of the Best Western Vernon Lodge Hotel & Conference Center. Debbie's journey allowed her to lead the hotel with a deep appreciation for all team members that filled each and every position. Every morning she'd start the day by visiting each department in the hotel to personally thank each of the seventy-plus employees for their presence that day. Debbie was forever committed to her routine because service was one of her highest values. She passed away some time ago, but her actions touched thousands of people. Her practice of recognizing and thanking others for their time continues to influence my choices to this day.

My life partner Tatiana is someone who continues to lead by example when it comes to serving. She's an incredibly disciplined, hard-working individual whose life purpose is dedicated to empowering other women. Tatiana works tirelessly behind the scenes, and she has the ability to easily identify strengths in people—oftentimes before they even recognize it within themselves. Many people struggle to see their own genius because they tend to focus on characteristics within themselves that society deems negative. Tatiana helps people see past these mental blocks, to rediscover their true self-expression and even lead in ways they never thought possible. She has a gift for identifying people who tend to feel invisible and often portray a tough demeanor to cover their inner pain. This ability allows her to quickly connect with people on a deep level, creating connections for self-discovery and, more importantly, for healing. I'm honored to share my life with someone who serves others by helping them reach their untapped potential.

Use your strengths to give with a higher purpose.

Years ago, when I was flat broke, one of my mentors at the time was kind enough to meet me at a local park. He was a very wealthy man who owned over 4,000 real estate properties, but you'd never know it by looking at him. He showed up to our meeting carrying a briefcase with a variety of newspapers and carefully cut out newspaper articles that we ended up reading over and then discussing. We came across an article in the *Morning Star* newspaper about a couple who had organized a hot dog sale to raise money for medical treatment and travel expenses on behalf of their son, who desperately needed to be flown to BC Children's Hospital in Vancouver, Canada. My mentor decided to contact the journalist who had written that article so he could contribute to this couple's cause. He took it a step further and used Vernon City Hall in British Columbia, Canada, as the return address from a numbered company so that the $10,000 CAD gift remained anonymous. One of the greatest things I learned from this man is, "The secret to living is giving." But keep it a secret when you can.

This encounter was largely responsible for opening my eyes to the power of giving. Through his good fortune my mentor not only helped a random family; he also taught me one of the most important lessons of my life—to give without expecting anything in return is the greatest symbol of wealth. There are endless opportunities for helping others as long as you have the empathy needed to truly *see* and *know* them. Empathy comes naturally to many people while others discover empathy later on in their lives through active learning and awareness. The beauty of empathy is that, just like any other skill, it gets easier the more often you practice.

Service has been at the top of my list of values for quite some time now. I've spent countless hours seeking out opportunities to bestow random acts of kindness on others. Time and time again, I've chosen to put my own needs and ego aside in order to understand the needs of others. Now, random acts of kindness are a natural extension of my daily life, wherein I constantly see opportunities to give, help, and serve.

When people go above and beyond the call of duty to serve me, I'm reminded of my higher purpose and return the favor. I've written letters to general managers, hotel owners, and other people in leadership roles recommending that their employees be considered for promotions or raises. For years now, I've made a point to diligently keep track of birthdays and remember to send birthday wishes to people every day. I continue to serve my connections and relationships by regularly sharing powerful and inspiring media online. It's my mission to inspire people through acts of kindness and generosity and my desire to take the world to greatness.

I once had an appointment to meet with a gentleman who had flown into Vancouver and was staying at the Fairmont Hotel in the airport. When I got there, he was watching CNN news with a pile of newspapers spread out in front of him. Confused and a little shocked, I asked him why he was studying all of it. He responded, "I don't know if you believe in God, Darren, but when I watch all of this negativity, that's God's to-do list. I don't look at it as negative news; rather, my mind begins strategizing to complete the list by solving problems and helping people." Although I don't know the specifics of how he accomplished this, I found the mindset behind this concept to be a complete shift from the way I once viewed things. Instead of approaching negative situations simply as bad, make the most of them by recognizing opportunity zones and finding ways to be of service to others as well as solve problems.

I've held a number of odd jobs throughout my life. This might sound strange to say, but I'm eternally grateful for every single one of these experiences. While working as a security officer for loss prevention, part of my job was to study and anticipate behavior before it occurred. During these seven years, I developed an acute ability to perceive when people were in dire need. Poverty was usually the cause of desperation in the people I would observe. To this day I'm still able to physically feel when people are struggling financially, and I'm very sensitive to the energy people give off when money is scarce. I just feel it. I pick up on it very easily, and it moves me. Now that I've achieved financial success, when I perceive such a situation, I frequently feel compelled to act on it. This is why I find it difficult to shop at brick-and-mortar stores during the holiday season.

When income grows, character also needs to grow.

In the past, I've been fortunate enough to anonymously cover grocery bills for people who were standing ahead of me in line. In these moments their energy was so strong, I could understand the fear that they were facing as they wondered whether or not their credit card would decline. Another way I've enjoyed surprising people has been by anonymously upgrading passengers who were on my same flight. While waiting at the gate, I'd sit and scan through people and then randomly pick someone I believed could use a nice surprise. Choosing men and women of all ages, I would then use my "Super Elite" status to upgrade these individuals. Once onboard I'd find the head flight attendant and ask them to upgrade a person's seat to business or first class. I can't begin to explain how thrilling it was to see the passengers' reactions when they found out they were being upgraded. There is so much joy and fulfillment in doing something for others, even while remaining anonymous.

VIPS

✔ The secret to living is giving. Enrich your life by putting the needs of others before your own.

✔ Some of the best acts of service can be entirely spontaneous, so be on the lookout for opportunities to give.

✔ Be a go-giver, not a go-getter.

✔ To give without expectation is the greatest symbol of wealth.

CHAPTER 2
INNOVATION

It's safe to say that much of my success in life has been fueled by a passionate desire to show all my doubters that I would succeed. From a young age I was determined to prove to the world that I was not weak or handicapped; rather, I was actually destined for a long and memorable life. Then, the thought of me actually having the ability to achieve these goals seemed far-fetched, yet many of my choices were influenced by this inner passion. My goal was to prove to everyone that I was, in fact, good enough. In high school, a guidance counselor and schoolteacher sat me down and told me I would have to repeat the twelfth grade. They referred to me as a "throwaway kid," and said I would most likely spend the rest of my life on welfare. At the time, their words shook my confidence, but I knew that if I worked hard, I could overcome their limiting beliefs of me. I've come to realize that even though childhood experiences affect each of us, we have the power to change the *direction* in which they propel us. Difficult experiences would often leave me broken for months on end. Perseverance, along with deliberate choices, allowed me to find purpose in the things that had once destroyed me. When I realized I could leverage both positive and negative energies, my life started moving in the right direction.

I wasn't always intentional or mindful about living according to the values in this book. For the most part, if something worked, then I kept moving in that direction. If not, I reconsidered my approach and came up with a new game plan. Throughout my life, innovation has been responsible for helping me escape darkness time and time again. This value has continually helped me find the courage to regain my footing. Throughout adolescence and early adulthood, I found myself flat broke most of the time and learned to rely heavily on Canada's "cash for recycling" system. As a kid, I'd pass the time ringing doorbells, asking people for their bottles and cans so I could exchange them for money to buy candy or other items to resell at school. I was able to reach my neighbors at opportune times by studying their schedules—everyone knew who I was and vice versa. The older I got, the more ambitious I became. Rather than asking for recycling, I began asking to borrow their lawnmower to cut their grass.

Cash flow was good thanks to my little lawncare hustle, so I decided to start my very own rent-a-kid business. In no time, I was the kid in the neighborhood with a reputation for getting paid to do odd jobs. My neighbor across the street at the time, Pat Smith, happened to be the Deputy Premier of Saskatchewan. Her husband was wheelchair-bound after a work-related accident, so for many years I would cut their grass and shovel their sidewalks. In an effort to grow my business, I asked her to write me an endorsement letter on official government letterhead. The next day I brought the letter to school with me and asked a secretary to help me print hundreds of photocopies. I put a copy into each of the newspapers that I delivered six days a week. If someone didn't receive newspapers, I'd slip a copy into their mailbox. Just like that, business was booming.

Whatever you lack in skill, make it up in numbers.

As I learned how to work smarter, not harder, I became more intentional about innovating and designing my ideal life. I began researching other entrepreneurs and came across the book *CASHFLOW Quadrant* by Robert T. Kiyosaki. This book proposes that there are two categories of people—those who trade their time for money and those who create or invest in assets that produce cash flow 24/7. Kiyosaki's diagram breaks this idea into four quadrants: Employee, Self-Employed,

Business Owner, and Investor. This concept shifted my mindset and completely changed my life when I realized I was personally living in the wrong quadrant. Some people are content with trading risky opportunities in exchange for security and stability. But that wasn't me. The way I saw it, I didn't have anything to lose, so why should I continue accepting the cost of being comfortable?

CASHFLOW Quadrant has had such a major impact on me that I invested in a high-quality printout of the diagram—one I continue to show to people on a regular basis.

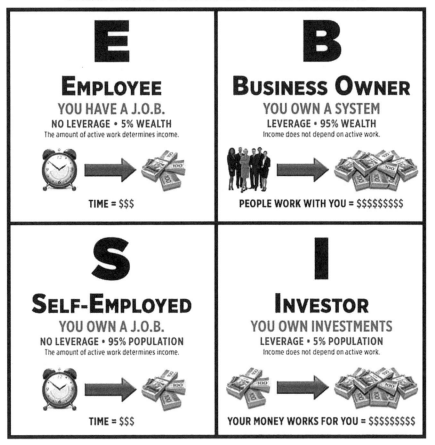

CASHFLOW QUADRANT
4 WAYS TO PRODUCE INCOME
LINEAR INCOME VS. LEVERAGED & RESIDUAL INCOME

E	**B**
EMPLOYEE	**BUSINESS OWNER**
YOU HAVE A J.O.B.	YOU OWN A SYSTEM
NO LEVERAGE • 5% WEALTH	LEVERAGE • 95% WEALTH
The amount of active work determines income.	Income does not depend on active work.
TIME = $$$	PEOPLE WORK WITH YOU = $$$$$$$$$
S	**I**
SELF-EMPLOYED	**INVESTOR**
YOU OWN A J.O.B.	YOU OWN INVESTMENTS
NO LEVERAGE • 95% POPULATION	LEVERAGE • 5% POPULATION
The amount of active work determines income.	Income does not depend on active work.
TIME = $$$	YOUR MONEY WORKS FOR YOU = $$$$$$$$$

I also own the CASHFLOW board game and regularly have people over once a month for a potluck game night. It's one of my go-to entertainment activities. As someone who's obsessed with personal development, I enjoy how this hands-on, collaborative game forces people to see themselves as part of a larger team. Kiyosaki's ideas opened my eyes to the world of investment opportunities and shaped my mindset into becoming the innovative thinker I am today.

Like many people, my financial report card has not always been one that I've been proud of. At times, I've been under such severe financial pressure that landlords have threatened to kick me out and change the locks for being so far behind on my rent. There were also several times I was at risk of having my cell phone or landline disconnected. I was backed into financial corners over and over again—until I reached an epiphany. It occurred to me that I had two choices: get really good at selling my personal belongings or get really good at selling a product or service. Rent was due in a few days, and I was cringing at the prospect of selling the things that mattered to me. So instead, I got creative and threw a block party.

Get good at selling a product or service or get good at selling your personal belongings.

I went around the neighborhood inviting everyone to the party that weekend. Without any food or drinks to offer, I decided to host a potluck and decorated the house as best I could. Unable to afford groceries, one of my goals was for the neighbors to leave behind any leftovers. When everyone showed up, I encouraged people to drink alcohol in order to cash in empty bottles and cans the next day. I loaded up the car the next morning, started the ignition, and noticed a little orange gas light on the dashboard staring back at me. Luckily, my house was situated at the top of a big hill. So, with zero gas in the tank, I managed to coast in neutral all the way down to a Petro-Canada gas station. I parked the car and went inside to let the attendant know I'd be back in a matter of minutes, ensuring my car wouldn't get towed. Then I grabbed the bags of bottles and cans and lugged them two blocks down to the recycling center. With the six dollars I received, I was able to put a little gas in the tank and make it back up the hill.

Now, with food and limited transportation again, I set to work on the last part of the massive block party plan. Over the next couple of days, I went around knocking on all the neighbors' doors who had stopped by and thanked them for attending. Then I offered to cut their grass, detail their car, wash their windows, or help them with any other odd job I could think of. My hustle paid off, and I was able to afford rent by the end of the month.

This situation taught me that money problems don't exist in life; there are only thinking problems. People often tend to focus on the doom and gloom side of obstacles, and the media typically doesn't help. But now I realize that problems often lead to opportunities. The reality is there's no lack of money in the world. Money is out there, it's just a matter of turning obstacles into cash flow. People struggle to make money because their thinking lacks innovation. As long as humanity encounters problems, there are opportunities to make money by solving them.

We don't have money problems; we have thinking problems.

Experience has taught me that we are each partially responsible for creating our own opportunities. When I started working toward a career as a corporate trainer, I became more in tune to innovative ideas to help me reach my goals. I soon realized that some of the visitors stopping by my house on a regular basis were actually points of contact for my target audience. Courier drivers working for large companies such as FedEx, UPS, and DHL were constantly coming and going. I focused on building relationships with these essential workers, giving them bottles of water and making a point to frequently chat with them. The longer I conversed with them, it became clearer that a few of them were gatekeepers to these companies. I would invite these courier drivers to potluck dinner parties that I hosted every couple of months. These simple conversations and gestures of kindness were actually helping me close the gap between myself and top-level executives.

In order to get my name and brand out there, I would host events featuring industry authorities, motivational speakers, and other special guests regardless of whether I had the money to do it. In these situations, I would book the conferences at relatively cheap hotels such as a Holiday Inn and ask to see the seminar room the night before. Then I'd ask to check out their back room for supplies such as extension cords and overhead projectors, stalling long enough in order for the hotel staff to leave me alone. Once they were gone, I'd return to the back room and sleep there because I was usually unable to afford an actual room. The next morning, I would use the lobby restroom to clean up, showering in the sinks and using the electric hand dryer to dry off. I would then change into the same suit from my high school graduation, which I continued to wear throughout the first ten years of my corporate training career.

In the mornings, before training, I would always make time to talk to the human resource managers in attendance. They usually had a corporate credit card or expense account, making them none too shy to buy me lunch that afternoon. This was how I was able to eat most days. I was ashamed of these secrets at the time, so I went to great lengths to hide them from everyone. I wanted to look good in front of others, never wanting anyone to suspect that I didn't have it all together. I was so worried of ruining my image that I did everything humanly possible to prevent anyone from ever finding out how I pulled it all off. Although at times I felt like a fake and a fraud, I knew that if I kept going, sheer numbers would have to account for some success.

Time will either *promote* you or *expose* you. It's just a matter of time.

Despite obstacles like these, the process of building my career as a corporate trainer was a lot of fun. Like a good magician, there are parts of my process I haven't shared with many people. For example, one of my tricks was to book a seat on a flight next to, or within close proximity to, an elusive potential client. This often took a bit of leg work like sifting through their inner circle to gather the details surrounding their travel plans. The detective work typically involved talking to a prospect's hairstylist, chiropractor, or close friend. Sealing the deal usually meant I had to sweet-talk flight attendants or other passengers. It's much easier to talk business with someone when they're stuck sitting next to you for an entire flight. This is exactly how I was able to meet Mark Victor Hansen when his book *Chicken Soup for the Soul* was taking off.

I learned a great deal from the mild stalking I did over the years, especially in regard to relationships. The relationships you form with others can either make it much easier or much harder for you to innovate your own destiny. One of my personal philosophies is that people don't care about how much we know—until they know how much we care about them. This is why I'm a compulsive notetaker. I pay close attention to other people's hobbies, goals, likes, dislikes, and points of interest, jotting down detailed notes about them under their contact cards on my cell phone. I have found that people are more receptive toward me once they realize I've made an effort getting to know them. Whenever I learn a fact about a friend, colleague, acquaintance, relative, team member, or someone even slightly close to my circle, I make a note of it. I've found that small details like these can potentially end up being a big deal down the line. Most people are happy to talk about themselves. The way I see it, people are constantly giving out clues about their life, and it's up to you to decide what to do with this information. The notes and clues I've collected often become relevant when I least expect it, so I do my best to listen intently during conversations rather than constantly thinking about my own responses.

People don't care about how much we know—until they know how much we care about them.

I heavily rely on my network of relationships, so I'm constantly looking to expand it. One of the walls in my office contains a board with a hundred photos of people I hope to meet. It includes John Travolta, Bill Gates, and the Dalai Lama. In my spare time I like to strategize different ways to materialize these important connections. I've found that one of the best methods is by physically placing myself in *opportunity zones*. This is a term I like to use in reference to hubs or hotspots of influential and powerful people. One of my go-to opportunity zones is the lounge at the Fairmont Hotel at Vancouver International Airport—even when I'm not traveling. If I'm at home and want to change my environment, focus on an abundance mindset, or increase my energy, I grab my laptop and head for the airport in search of opportunities to engage with high-level business individuals or entrepreneurs. After all, if people don't know you, they can't cash flow you.

By placing yourself in close proximity to people who are more likely to benefit from your services, you are thereby placing yourself in a position of power. People like to buy, but they don't like to be sold. I'd like to share with you what I've learned about the value of prequalifying your potential audience. I used to attend trade shows and "broke" networking events—gatherings of people who have no money and are looking for potential clients. Unfortunately, I didn't fully understand the world I was stepping into, approaching my first shows with naïve optimism. I would charge my admission to the trade show on my credit card even though I had no real money to pay it back. However, I did have thirty days to come up with the money. I figured, among the thousands of people in attendance, I was bound to meet and close with enough people to make the credit card payment before it was due. It was crushing to realize that none of these people were prequalified to buy my product or service. They had zero interest in it and worse, no money to pay for it—period. The lesson here is to make sure you're speaking to the *right* audience before you invest in them. By shifting my focus to an audience with disposable income—rather than one with paycheck-to-paycheck mentality—my results also began to change.

Your network equals your net worth.

If you want to achieve at a level higher than most, then you must innovate habits that are more effective than most. I've found it extremely helpful to block out time on my calendar for wealth-building activities. "Passive Income Planning" is color-coded green in my agenda. I focus solely on generating revenue during this block of time. When I first created this habit, I had to practice conscious discipline. Over time though, it became effortless to focus on texts, calls, emails, and brainstorming. This practice indeed propelled me to reach my financial goals faster. What are some habits you can create that will bring you more of the things you want in life?

I acknowledge innovation to be one of my strengths as well as one of my core values. For this reason, I consider myself to be extremely fortunate. Most people are also capable of being innovative thinkers. It just requires focus, deliberate action, and a little faith.

VIPs

✔ We have the power to choose in which direction our childhood experiences propel us.

✔ Money is out there, it's just a matter of finding a way to turn obstacles into cash flow.

✔ Having the mindset of an innovator can help you recognize opportunities to solve countless problems, which can in turn translate to a bigger bank account.

✔ If you're feeling stuck in life, consider placing yourself in an *opportunity zone*—a place where you're surrounded by people who are more likely to benefit from your services.

✔ If you wish to be in close proximity to money that has already been made, then focus your energy on innovating connections and relationships. Once in this position, you can then leverage opportunities to grow and scale far more quickly than if you had simply focused your energy on making money alone. Work smarter, not harder.

Meeting Dr. John Gray who famously explained relationships in his book *Men Are From Mars, Women Are From Venus*—people like Gray have sustained Darren's continued growth

Pay it forward—the best way to learn something is to teach it to others

Life is about creating experiences and memories

Darren meeting one of his biggest influencers, Dr. John Demartini

CHAPTER 3

ABUNDANCE

There was a farmer who grew excellent quality corn. Every year he won the award for the best grown corn. One year a newspaper reporter interviewed him and learned something interesting about how he grew it. The reporter discovered that the farmer shared his seed corn with his neighbors. "How can you afford to share your best seed corn with your neighbors when they are entering corn in a competition with yours each year?" the reporter asked.

"Why, sir," said the farmer. "Didn't you know? The wind picks up the pollen from the ripening corn and swirls it from field to field. If my neighbors grow inferior corn, cross-pollination will steadily degrade the quality of my corn. If I am to grow good corn, I must help my neighbors grow good corn."

So is with our lives…those who want to live meaningfully and well must help enrich the lives of others, for the value of a life is measured by the lives it touches. And those who choose to be happy must help others find happiness, for the welfare of each is bound up with the welfare of all.

—Unknown

At a young age, I adopted an opinion about the world and life that would prevent me from growing and succeeding for many years. I never made a conscious decision to have a scarcity mindset, but rather, it came about as a result of the environment in which I was raised. My understanding of the world was the false notion that it was like a fixed-size pie, made of limited resources and opportunities. I used to believe that when someone took a piece of this pie, fewer resources were left for everyone else. In turn, the success of another person was a threat to my own. Instead of celebrating others' accomplishments, I would begrudgingly turn inward to punish myself for letting someone steal *my* chance at a better life yet again. There's a popular saying we've all heard that money doesn't grow on trees. This is an example of the restrictive thinking that is ingrained in many of us as small children. It teaches us that money is hard to come by, a belief that once made it impossible for me to build my dream life until I replaced it with a new concept—the truth.

The reality is that we live in a world of abundance. Many people don't see it this way because the human brain is hardwired for survival, meaning we have a tendency to view each other as competitors fighting for the same things. We are constantly searching for ways to advance more, earn more, and become more, all in a very turbulent world. My life started moving in a better direction when I recognized that I was stuck, smack-dab in the middle of all this turbulence because my mindset was rooted in lack and scarcity. I realized that if I wanted to rise above the problems that overshadowed me, I would have to reconstruct many parts in my flawed belief system. This process required me to deny my very nature. It would involve giving up my ego and reprogramming my conscious and unconscious mind to let go of the thoughts that had given me a false sense of safety and comfort. I had to make a habit of pausing and checking my awareness of the thoughts going through my head. I had to repeat new mantras to myself such as "Those who succeed do not take away from me" and "A closed door is just *one* closed door." By implementing these new habits, little by little, a better version of Darren began to appear.

As I shifted and settled into my new abundance mindset, I began realizing just how destructive my old thoughts had been. It became clear that I was regularly creating my own source of stress. I used to read restaurant menus from right to left, viewing the price before the meal itself. I wasted an inordinate amount of time driving around looking for the cheapest gas or hotel and then, after giving up in frustration, occasionally I just ended up sleeping in my car. I would only buy groceries and essential items that were on sale. Then one day, I realized I didn't want to live this way anymore. Instead, I wanted to have the means to place a food order based on my appetite instead of the cost, to fill up my tank at the closest station regardless of the price, and to make necessary purchases without second-guessing my spending. Sick of always coming up short-handed, I decided to reconsider my thinking. Rather than focusing on the same thoughts that kept me locked in a mindset of lack and scarcity, I reinvested my time into learning how to create more money. I soon discovered the ability to see beyond my circumstances and combat scarcity with prosperity.

Just because one person succeeds does not mean that another must fail.

After finding myself homeless for a short period of time and sleeping in an apple orchard, I came to the difficult realization that no one was coming to save me. I used to fantasize about the day when a relative, the lottery, or maybe even the government would find and rescue me. But that day never came. In order to do better and be better, I needed to stop playing the role of a victim and instead adopt the practice of intentionality. We are all plagued by blind spots. Whether you live in a mansion or in your car, it's difficult to envision a different life for yourself. The first step of living with intentionality is having clarity, which is why many people find it easier to sit back and let life happen to them. People often struggle to envision a better life for themselves simply because their scarcity mindset keeps them from fully seeing what *could* be. The circumstances into which we're born do not need to define our entire lives. The world holds an abundance of opportunity. We have the power to change as much as we need to so that the doors to our success may open.

Problems are inevitable in life. We're all either coming from a problem, in a problem, or headed toward a problem. Only when you change your mindset toward abundance, do you start seeing these problems as opportunity zones. Instead of getting caught off guard and reacting to every crisis, you begin responding to situations simply by asking yourself what you'll do with them. Instead of being a negative trigger, the problem then becomes an opportunity from which you get to create a solution. Our problems are actually an indicator of our growth. When we encounter newer and bigger issues, this is a sign that we are leveling up, or skilling up, in life. The more successful we become in life, the larger our problems will be. Oftentimes you'll find that you don't have the skills to come up with solutions on your own. This is the point at which many people stay stuck. They don't reach out for help, or they reach out to the wrong people for help. The people in your inner circle likely have the same problems as you or worse. The key is to reach *outside* your inner circle and find people who can truly help you.

An abundance mindset can set you free, but you're the only one capable of turning this opportunity into something great.

Finding success requires a few steps. For me, some of these have come naturally. Not because they were easy but because I had no choice. Much of my early life was do or die, a mentality which lends itself to the risk-taking that is much needed throughout the pursuit of entrepreneurship. There was a turning point in my career, before I achieved success as an entrepreneur, where I was fortunate to have experienced a second epiphany. In this moment I realized that there's no shortage of people available to talk about your product or services. There are billions of people on the planet who are capable of promoting what you're selling, as long as you are willing to take the first steps. You must *believe* in yourself and be an advocate for the things you *believe in*. Otherwise, no one will. You must be able to overcome plenty of rejection, and in my experience, this comes from having an abundance mindset. One *no* does not mean every *no*. There are billions of possible *yes'* out there if you can determine the right approach.

I'm a lifelong fan of the American rock band Chicago. They stopped in Vancouver during a tour, and their concert was sold out within a matter of minutes. One of my favorite bands of all time was in town to perform at the Pacific National Exhibition, but there were zero tickets left. I wasn't going to take no for an answer. I showed up at the event eight hours early with a plan—I would meet with the CEO of the event himself. About an hour later, he found me waiting at the box office and explained that there was nothing he could do, as the event had sold out months ago. Deciding it was still too early in the game to accept defeat, I started brainstorming. I watched people arrive for the concert and realized that statistically speaking, some of the ticketholders simply wouldn't make it to the show. I knew I still had a chance, so I sat by the booth and waited. A couple of people working the event noticed my little protest, and I explained to them that I wasn't going to leave unless I had tickets to the concert. A few minutes after showtime, I was thrilled to see these same people return with a ticket for me in hand. This will forever be one of my top favorite musical performances, especially because my seat was in the very front row. One *no* does not mean every *no*.

At some point while reading this book, you've probably thought to yourself, *Darren, this is great and all, but I still don't understand how to replicate this in my own life.* How do you believe in yourself when you've lived with the same brain, the same thoughts, the same doubts for so long? For starters, let me explain that if it was possible for me, then it's possible for you too. There are very few people in this world who fall into the same category that I did when I was approaching high school graduation. There's a high probability that you were never told you wouldn't survive past the age of twenty-one or that you would live off welfare for the rest of your life. If you *did* happen to hear these words *and* you've managed to read this far, then I'd say you're absolutely moving in the right direction.

So how does a person passionately and unquestionably believe in themselves? One of the most helpful tools, in my experience, has been to turn my focus toward my inner child. Generally speaking, inner child work involves addressing and healing the wounds that you've harbored since childhood. Many people find this type of work to be life-changing, and I would encourage anyone to further explore it. However, I'd like to share a different approach to inner child work. In the eyes of children, life is a game. Children are endlessly playful and always seem to create games out of nearly every situation. It's in their nature to jump right in without hesitation. They have not yet experienced enough of the failure, embarrassment, or disappointment that causes most adults to live in fear. On the other hand, most adults take themselves out of the game before it has even begun. Their mindset and self-talk keep them from imagining all the fulfilling and fun ways there are to win, so they lack the courage to even show up. Most people show up in in their lives the way they show up for a pick-up game. Many of those who *do* show up, just play casually because they're afraid of committing to something that might end poorly.

Don't take yourself out of the game before the game has even begun.

I would like to challenge you to look inside yourself and find the unapologetic perseverance that lives within your inner child. There is an abundance of creative energy inside each of us—energy that can push us to discover the focus, drive, and inspiration we often can't seem to find otherwise. We are all capable of fusing this inner child energy with the wisdom and understanding of our adult mind. As adults, we have to accept the reality that average effort leads to an average life. Average focus brings about average results. I've admittedly struggled to maintain focus throughout the course of my life. I now believe in the power of manifestation, or the idea that "when the intention is clear, the results will appear."

The key is to welcome abundance into your life and allow it to feed the roots of things you wish to manifest. Most people are misled to believe in the following process: have, then do, then become. They think metamorphosis begins with tangible changes. I have successfully reprogrammed my thinking and consciously abide by a different process: be, then do, then have. The process of becoming someone new or different starts with the mind, so I visualize myself in the situation I desire and believe it wholeheartedly. My actions then align as though I have already achieved my vision. This is the process that allows me to achieve my goals in life.

If you had asked me a year ago whether I could ever hike over 60 miles or 100 km a week, I would have said, "It's not going to happen." It wasn't until I started putting my process to practice that I truly believed it was possible. Once I started seeing results, releasing weight, and experiencing increased energy, this "do" became a major focus in my life—a non-negotiable, scheduled commitment. I started eating better and challenging myself to daily hikes of increased distances, and I actually looked forward to measuring my progress. To keep myself accountable, I have created a hiking group. This support team creates an environment of like-minded people who share similar goals. Most people fail because they fail to plan. One day I decided that I would be a healthier, stronger, and more physically powerful version of myself. Now, I have become a regular hiker and look forward to reaching summits all over the world.

I'd like you to picture someone living in a big city such as Dallas or Los Angeles. This person just obtained a real estate license for the first time and is excited to begin their new career, until they discover that there are thousands of other realtors already working in their city. Their thoughts begin racing, the scarcity mindset invades, and they begin to seriously doubt that they'll ever make it to their initial vision of success. Thick clouds creep over their outlook, and they begin to lose sight of their intention. They've taken themselves out of the game before it has even begun simply by thinking it so. Now, imagine that same person, recognizing the thousands of realtors, acknowledging the temporary intimidation but then choosing to focus on their own game. They waste little time with doubt and instead concentrate their energy on becoming the best in class and achieving faster results. These hypothetical scenarios happen in real life, every day. Which path will you choose?

You have the power to control your negativity.

In 2001, I set out to put together one hell of a vision board. I was living in Vernon, British Columbia, Canada, and decided to take a personal development course, which was being presented about a four-hour drive from my home. It started raining on my way back from the course, and I ended up getting lost somewhere in the Vancouver lower mainland. Through the rain, I saw a giant, impressive mansion. I turned the car around and headed back to the closest convenience store to purchase a disposable camera. Returning to the formidable "home," I snapped a photo. When I finally found my way back, I printed the picture and fixed it onto my growing vision board.

That photo sat on my wall for a very long time, and as the years went by, my hopes of one day living in a mansion started to dwindle. I started thinking that the image would end up being nothing more than a source of inspiration. Then I met a woman through a volunteer program that I had been involved with at the time. She turned out to be the groundskeeper of the very same mansion that had been sitting on my vision board for the past six years. It just so happened that she was looking for someone to live on-site for insurance purposes. *Six years* after taking the original picture, I found myself living full-time in that 14,000 square-foot mansion, rent-free.

Do you admit to having a scarcity mindset? It's okay! Even if it's discouraging, take a moment to fully own this reality. Now, let's focus on more actions that will help you break free from this heavy burden that's been hindering your growth. It has been extremely helpful for me to be intentional about my surroundings. Much of the media spews out messages of doom, gloom, scarcity, and pessimism, so it's a good idea to limit your exposure to it. I mentioned in the last chapter that I physically place myself in environments of opportunity such as the Fairmont or the Four Seasons. If you don't already do this, I implore you to step out of your comfort zone and give it a shot. If this thought scares you, rest assured it used to freak me out too! Digging deep and pushing yourself to be uncomfortable can keep you engaged in an abundance mindset. Don't wait for hope to find you—create your own.

Another way to move past lack and scarcity is to surround yourself with people who are generally more established. When I was young and doing odd jobs through my rent-a-kid business, I would often chat with my customers inside their homes to better understand their path to success. A mentor and close friend of mine used this approach as early as high school. He would evaluate his friends' parents, seeking mentors who could pull him up as they succeeded in life. He grew close to many of these people who became fond of his energy, enthusiasm, and thirst for a better life. He brought value to them by way of his positive attitude and work ethic. In return, his successful, more experienced friends lifted him up as they rose higher and higher. This was Tony Jeary, now known as The RESULTS Guy™.

Tony applied the lessons he learned from an early age and now sits at the top of a multi-million-dollar organization, advising many of the world's top authorities. Not too long ago, I flew out of DFW to meet with Tony. He could have easily arranged to have an uber or a taxi pick me up, but instead Tony sent his RESULTS1 Van. This fully equipped, custom Sprinter van is designed to be an office on the go. As someone who's highly intentional about their environment, I greatly appreciated the gesture.

Befriend people who embody the things you wish to emulate.

There are plenty of opportunities in the world to surround yourself with abundance. The problem is that most people don't have the curiosity needed to get out and look for these opportunities. I've been curious about the luxury lifestyle for as long as I can remember. My interest went so far as to knock on doors in affluent neighborhoods, asking people how they came about their wealth. Tatiana and I have been dreaming of flying private for a while now, so we recently decided to go on a date to the private charter terminal at Vancouver International Airport. We spent the majority of a day touring a private jet and experiencing what it feels like to live at a higher level of freedom. The jet was grounded the entire time, yet our intention was to physically place ourselves within the dream. Our date was a way for us to dream build and to strengthen our intention.

Tatiana and I believe in having dreams and goals. We do not believe in sitting around, hoping for the stars to align. Both of us continue to work hard to overcome the blind spots we developed early on in our lives. We seek out and have taken many training and development courses to help us discover our blind spots. Take it from us—it's nearly impossible to uncover blinds spots on your own because they are among the things you don't know that you don't know. Our decision to live with an abundance mindset has transformed our lives, both individually and as a couple, uniting us in the process. We wish the same for you.

VIPs

- ✔ Remember, no one is coming to rescue you.
- ✔ In life, you are either coming from a problem, in a problem, or heading toward a problem.
- ✔ BE, DO, and then HAVE.
- ✔ Your environment is always stronger than your willpower. Hence the importance of choosing the right environment.
- ✔ Seek mentors, training, and development opportunities to help you discover your blind spots.

CHAPTER 4

FUN

Over the years, I've met an enormous amount of people. Based on what I've witnessed and experienced in these countless interactions, I feel sure in saying that people tend to focus on success as a destination rather than on the journey itself. They generally think that happiness will come when they finally have the house on a hill or that promotion they've been tirelessly working toward. Though I admire the work ethic and relentless dedication of these individuals, I feel like they end up sacrificing too much of the incredible lives we are each given. Tomorrow is never guaranteed. There's no assurance you'll see the light of morning or even wake up as the same able-bodied person you hopefully are today. That being said, I believe in working hard and celebrating often. Playfulness and joy are natural parts of life; animals and children are a testament to this truth. Remember the inner child concept I discussed in the last chapter? Well, we all carry that part of ourselves until the day we pass on. The kid inside of us serves as a reminder that it's important to laugh, celebrate, and have fun!

By now you've probably gathered that I live a pretty intentional life. My days are usually planned in great detail with calendar color-coding, icons, and little reminders all over. I have time blocked out for passive income brainstorming sessions, master planning my life, and revenue-generating activities. I have a one-page yearly plan, a quarterly plan, monthly plans, weekly plans, and daily plans. So it shouldn't come as a surprise that I make sure to schedule time for plenty of fun.

It's important for me to have events and activities to look forward to. Although I consider myself a unique person, I'm positive this is not something specific to me alone. Everyone needs to regain balance after putting in the time that work demands of us. For those of us with hectic schedules, it's a good idea to plan ahead for a time when you'll inevitably need to restore that balance.

Traveling is one of my favorite ways to squeeze fun into my buzzing schedule. I can't express how much I love experiencing life in different parts of the world. Exploring new places allows me to get out of my head for a little while and get back in touch with the big picture. Revisiting familiar places gives me a sense of nostalgia and comfort. The Okanagan Valley in British Columbia, Canada, is one of my favorite places to visit. There are many activities such as hiking, boating, skiing, wine tasting, and visiting the many farmers' markets. I particularly enjoy the lifestyle of the people in the area. It's a slower pace that makes every day feel like you're on vacation. I'm lucky to live in a city that's big enough for me to explore like a tourist, even after twenty-one years. The lifestyle of Vancouver never fails to inspire me. I'll never get tired of sitting by the harbor watching float planes land and take off, seeing enormous yachts cruise by in all their glory, and hiking the endless trails in the North Shore.

I really enjoyed pretending to be a tourist throughout the short while I lived in San Francisco. Sometimes I would treat myself to a weekend staycation at the Fairmont. Many of my best memories happened on a rental bike, simply riding around the pier and the surrounding city. Before the days of smartphones, I would wander out with no map and no particular place in mind. One day I ventured out so far that I ended up having to get directions back to the hotel. I've never been so happy to get lost in my entire life. I spent that whole day stopping at different restaurants, cafes, events, and scenic lookouts. Each time I went somewhere new, I'd ask a stranger to suggest a recommendation for my next stop. Many of the people I approached were a little reserved at first, but after some chit chat, they seemed genuinely invested in my desire for fun and adventure. As someone who generally lives according to a set schedule, it was refreshing to just sit back and let an entire day unravel organically before me. I felt a natural high from the emotions and energy that came from not knowing where I'd end up next. To this day, I continue to chase that same feeling.

I'm fortunate enough to have the means to enjoy sailing, concerts, musical clubs, and Broadway shows. I don't personally own any supercars because it's hard for me to justify the cost and expensive upkeep, yet the speed and engineering fascinate me. The best part of fun is that it doesn't always have to be a big, overpriced ordeal. Fun is subjective, so my experiences may or may not resonate with you. They might serve as examples for you, or you might think they're downright weird. Public speaking, for instance, is something I genuinely look forward to. However, I'm well aware that for some, it's right at the top of their list of biggest fears and a far cry from what they would consider to be fun.

Become your own source of fun.

Dream building is one of my more low-key pastimes. Private jets are a recent obsession, and my goal is to be flying private within the next five years. Over the last few weeks, before bedtime, I've been watching related YouTube videos. One video featured a guy who had just obtained his jet and hired a film crew to document and put together a thirty-minute montage of his experience. The video captured every detail, from pulling up to the airline, getting the keys to the plane, to meeting his pilots. I love little videos like this because they give me the chance to live vicariously, through other people, reenacting their experiences in my spirit until I'm able to materialize them in my own life.

I am incredibly lucky to live in a part of the world where I'm surrounded by woods, thousands of nature trails, and especially Stanley Park. Birds migrate back to Vancouver in the spring, so I've enjoyed listening to the sounds of new birds in the area. There's always an abundance of things to see and learn from nature. Our environment serves as a reminder to slow down, observe, and stay present. Little moments like sunrises, sunsets, light conversations with strangers, being around empowering people who share my values, taking in the world around me—these are just a few of the small things that make me feel wealthier than money ever could.

A few years ago, I flew out to Uganda, East Africa, for a humanitarian trip. I was thrilled because my plan was to stay with a small tribe in a mud hut for a couple of days, which to me, sounded like the ultimate foreign experience. I haven't met too many people who would be excited to sleep on a dirt floor, but I was freaking excited. When my guide and I approached the village, I was surprised to see that no one was wearing clothes. The thought of being surrounded by naked strangers instantly made me uncomfortable, so the initial round of introductions was pretty awkward. Shortly after, my translator said, "They would like to know why you feel the need to wear a costume." I looked down at my outfit and realized that they viewed our western clothing as a costume and completely unnecessary. My translator continued, "Why don't you just be authentic and fully free? Why do you have to wear these things from a manufactured plant and cover yourself with them? What are you hiding?"
Oh my gosh.

Their observations and perspectives shattered many of the assumptions I had lived with for so long; nevertheless, I politely chose to keep my clothes on. I spent the next couple of days with no electricity or running water, eating crickets and grasshoppers, with a group of naked strangers in an African village. To this day, it was some of the most fun I've ever had. At nighttime the darkness surrounded us like thick black curtains, and our massive bonfire was the only source of light for miles. After the fact, I learned how big these fires were; I bet you could actually see them from the International Space Station. Each night we danced around the fire and celebrated the fact that we got to live to see another day—it was intoxicating. I had never before experienced this surreal sensation of feeling drunk on the sheer life force and energy around me. My wish is that all people get to experience what it feels like to be as fully alive as I did during my trip. To be free from judgment, guilt, shame, filters, or concern for outward appearance. To be fully self-expressed.

My trip to Uganda helped me realize that humans really don't need much to have fun. The people of this tribe had absolutely nothing, yet they were the most blissfully happy people living their lives exactly as they were. Forget about careers, academic achievement, money, institutions, and fame because none of this creates happiness. The tribe helped me see the world in a new way. I realized that before this trip, I unknowingly had an ethnocentric mindset. This led me to make false assumptions about cultural differences. I would use norms from my culture to generalize about other peoples' cultures and customs. Without being consciously aware, I would use my culture as a universal yardstick—which caused me to be way off base and misjudge other people. In the end, thinking ethnocentrically resulted in my reducing another culture's way of life to a version of my own. Seeing this blind spot, I have learned that cultural misinterpretation can distort communication between human beings of different cultures. I'm beyond lucky to have had the chance to deeply connect with these people and learn this important lesson about the art of living.

Trade your expectations for appreciation, and your life will change in amazing ways.

One of the common regrets people have when they're dying is that they wish they hadn't worked so hard. We live in a society that values the treadmill of work, which can be a slippery slope. I think real success happens when you're able to build a career around something you find fun and truly enjoy. Many people understand the importance of living with gratitude and appreciation for life, and yet, this is so much easier to do when you're *actually* happy to be alive. You know yourself better than anyone else in the world, so take a moment and forget about what everyone else thinks. Ask yourself whether or not your days bring you joy and fulfillment. Ask yourself whether or not you're having enough fun. If your answer is no, then I encourage you to seek out a lifestyle that inspires you, so that when the sun sets, you can't wait to celebrate the fact that you got to live to see another day. In the words of Jane Marczweski, "You can't wait until life isn't hard anymore before you decide to be happy."

VIPs

✔ Don't just wait for fun to happen, schedule fun into your life and make it happen.

✔ Create a live list to do things now, instead of a bucket list planned for the end of your life.

✔ Learn to embrace the present moment and celebrate the simple things in life.

✔ Remember to always tell your face to smile.

✔ Speed is calculated by miles per hour, but life is calculated as smiles per hour. If you want extra mileage in life, simply smile more.

CHAPTER 5
RELATIONSHIPS

I believe in measuring the things that matter. Relationships typically play an essential role in many of my other values, which means they definitely matter. Being of service to others frequently leads to the strengthening of existing relationships as well as to the formation of new ones. Innovation often begins with looking to more accomplished people for inspiration and direction. An abundance mindset has everything to do with the relationship you have with yourself, and fun is absolutely better when it's a shared experience. The idea of measuring your relationships might sound a little funny, but strategic approaches can be helpful even when it comes to connecting with others.

I have learned to measure business relationships based on two metric categories—effective versus ineffective and relational versus transactional. We train our team members to be go-givers rather than go-getters because our results consistently support this approach. As a team, we study these metrics twice weekly. This game we've developed around relationship building keeps us motivated to meet people in ways that are both effective and genuinely relational. Our game also creates culture, community, and comradery within the team.

I've always been obsessed with wanting to meet different people to find out who they are and what makes them tick. People are endlessly fascinating to me, and thinking about all the different walks of humanity excites me. The excitement of meeting someone new can make me chatty, so I'm intentional about measuring my interactions with the eighty-twenty rule. I let the other person talk eighty percent of the time while doing my best to limit my talking to twenty percent. This pushes me to focus on asking thoughtful questions that keep the other person talking about the experiences and qualities that make them unique. I go back to this rule over and over again because it's tough to listen when you're doing all of the talking. Listening is vital to understanding what a person might need. This last piece is crucial because one of the best ways of building relationship equity is by helping someone in need.

The rationale behind relationship equity is that a connection between two people becomes more valuable when contributions are made by each person. This principle works because most people feel naturally inclined to seek the balance of equal give and take. I'm not proposing that you should do nice things for people simply because you're likely to get something in return. I'm sharing this with you because understanding human nature leads to stronger and longer-lasting relationships. Equity can also quickly build trust between two people. Everyone is different. Some people need a short period of time to trust another, whereas others need several weeks or even years. As a corporate trainer, trust is an important part of building relationships with my clients. I've said this before, and I'll say it again—people don't care about what we know until they know how much we care about them. Some of my biggest wins began by showing a potential or existing client that I have a genuine desire to see *them* win.

Network, listen, serve, and then build.

Traveling has been a huge part of my career. Each year I would host hundreds of seminars and meetings at various hotels internationally. I settled into routines using many of the same hotels over and over again, so much that the hotel staff became an extension of my own customer service team. When clients came out to conferences and events, they were always greeted first and foremost by a member of the hotel team. If they needed help finding the training room or needed directions to the restrooms, a concierge or desk attendant would show them the way.

As soon as I came to this realization, I knew I had to double-down on creating relationship equity with each and every hotel staff member.

One of the ways I succeeded in building these relationships was by acknowledging employees and thanking them with handwritten letters. It wasn't long before everyone knew me on a first-name basis, at which point I could trust that my visiting clients would be well taken care of. Seminars were running more smoothly than ever, yet I still felt a desire to give back and do more for my unofficial team members. When staff went above and beyond the roles and responsibilities of their job descriptions, I would draft a letter to the hotel's upper management in recognition of the employees. I used these letters to spotlight individuals as key assets that ought to be taken care of; otherwise, they might be recruited elsewhere. My messages encouraged higher ups to reward these deserving team members with raises, promotions, and other forms of recognition.

Over the years, I saw many of the entry-position workers graduate to supervisory, management, and even executive positions. We grew together, as one big team, and so did our relationships. One night before a big conference, I checked into one of my usual spots, only to find out that the hotel had been overbooked; even the sister properties were oversold. I had to be onsite the next morning, and things weren't looking good. That is, until a familiar face appeared behind the desk. A shift manager recognized me as the customer whose handwritten letter had helped her get a promotion earlier that year. She greeted me with a smile, and I let out a sigh of relief. Thanks to our relationship equity, my reservation was upgraded to the presidential suite that night, at no additional cost. You never know just how far a ripple of impact will go.

Tony Jeary developed and teaches a concept called *Life Team*, which neatly sums up my experiences. He believes that there are select people—in both our professional and personal lives—who shape and affect us in ways greater than most. These people come from different life categories, including business, spiritual, home, and health. They often provide us with inspiration and encouragement, giving us guidance or information to help us make better decisions. Tony suggests that a good way to acknowledge and appreciate these people is by building your *Life Team* around them. My world improved drastically the instant I recognized all the hotel staff members as being part of my own *Life Team*. Take a moment to consider the people who influence your life the most. Do these people support you? Do they believe in your dreams? Do they make you a better person? Lastly, what do they have to say about you?

In basic terms, the corporate world is a business of relationships and people. In life, everything we want, need, or desire comes from strangers. Experience has shown me that a big part of what I do begins simply by bridging the gap between strangers. Once in place, this bridge gives me access to a greater network, and it is through this network of conversations that I'm able to help companies reach greater heights. Many people, however, choose to do life alone, much like I used to. They don't have a *Life Team*, and they're not stepping into new conversations on a regular basis. These people often wonder why their life lacks abundance. I've heard some of them defend their choices by saying that making connections goes against their personality. They often label themselves as introverts and assume nothing can be done about it. Then again, I've seen these same people transform their lives and flourish by letting go of a belief system they've carried around for far too long. The corporate world revolves around relationships and people, but so does the rest of the world.

A big part of my role as a corporate trainer also involves uncovering a company's blind spots, underutilized assets, and monetization opportunities. The next step is to connect the right people under the right circumstances, to help them scale their company, expand through mergers and acquisitions, or establish strategic joint ventures. The right opportunity zones can lead to big wins for myself and for my clients, though it's important to note that the clients with whom I choose to engage also become part of my opportunity zones. I have to be extremely selective about who I choose to work with and invite into my inner circle. Jim Treliving once said, "I make decisions about work with my heart, about money with my head, and about people with my gut." I couldn't have said it better myself.

Experience has taught me that relationships suffer the most when people become too attached to the outcome. Society has a lot to say about the way relationships should be, especially romantic ones. Couples often move quickly through the steps of commitment because they're too focused on marriage as the ultimate outcome. The pressure that builds in these relationships usually leads to pain and heartbreak. Some people only engage in relationships because they have an agenda and want something specific from the other person. It's rare for these people to get what they really want because humans are all connected through energy. The energy of our intent is a lot like a boomerang; if you toss one while focusing entirely on the outcome, then it's probably not going to come back.

I've already mentioned the importance of surrounding yourself with the right people to inspire you and create opportunity zones— especially with people who have done the deal. It's equally important to develop quality relationships with these people. In most cases, your net worth mirrors the levels of your five closest friends. Our friends influence our outlook, motivation level, emotions, values, and so much more. As I said before, we are all connected through energy. It's up to

Our relationships define the quality of our lives.

us to protect our own energy and vision. We can do so by selectively choosing who we allow to be a part of our lives on a deeper, more intimate level. Surround yourself with like-minded friends with whom you can build relationship equity. There's a group I hang out with on a regular basis near the boating area in front of Stanley Park. I've learned innumerable lessons about life and business from this like-minded group, which I continue to leverage in my own life. I'm also involved with a travel community of people from all over the world and a hiking community, which I meet up with every Sunday. It's important to have different groups or communities for the areas of interest in your life because collective knowledge will always be greater than just your own.

Wherever I go, I always make a point to say hello to people around me. Our relationships define the quality of our lives. It's not about the number of relationships you have; rather, it's all about getting to know people, spending time with them, and building trust. You never know how or when the people you meet today may play a role in your future later in life. Even if you're currently working as an employee, years from now you might find yourself owning or overseeing an entire business. It's entirely possible that you could end up working with the people you meet today. We cannot predict how people are going to show up and influence our lives, which is why we should value each relationship. Many people spend time with others and get to know them simply out of necessity. In these situations, as soon as the transaction or deal is complete, the relationship fades away. Out of sight, out of mind. In my experience, it's better to keep channels of communication and friendship open whenever possible, so consider taking the time to foster long-term relationships that outlast the lifetime of whatever circumstances brought you together in the first place. Follow up with each other because, again, you never know what the future holds.

I'd like to share some of the most influential relationships from my life. It was an honor to be friends with the late Bill Bartmann, who was a billionaire from the United States.

Bill cared deeply about other people, including every one of his 3,900 employees. He was incredibly charitable, yet my favorite thing about Bill was the fact that, despite his enormous wealth, he kept it real. His favorite restaurant was International House of Pancakes. He'd choose IHOP over a fancy steakhouse any day, and I loved him for it. Bill's style was always casual, sporting jeans and a t-shirt whenever he could get away with it. Many people at his level of wealth would travel with an entourage. However, Bill's impacts were high while his profile stayed low. He looked like any other down-to-earth guy walking down the street, blending right in with the crowd. He even drove himself around in a pre-owned GMC Jimmy four-by-four truck. Best described as approachable, humble, and generous with his time, Bill cared deeply about his employees and about making a difference in the world. Our friendship shattered many of the preconceptions I'd held toward billionaires and gave me insights about the way people ought to be treated. I stopped seeing them as untouchable people and instead began treating everyone fairly and equally.

The relationship I have with Dr. John Demartini has also influenced me personally and changed my way of thinking. John has an incredible way of practicing generational thinking and planning into the future. I swear the guy thinks a thousand years ahead. He's the person who inspired me to create a 250-year legacy plan for my family foundation. My friendship with John opened my mind and allowed me to think about human behavior at an entirely new level. Thank you, John, for changing me for the better.

I'd also like to thank Tony Jeary, for taking me to the next level. Tony has mastered the art of paying attention to details. Working closely with him has given me the opportunity to see just how thoughtfully and intentionally he operates his business and life. The van I was picked up in was impeccable, the washrooms were spotless, and not a pen was out of place. Shortly after meeting him, I received a welcome kit in the mail that blew me away. Tony has a talent for building relationship equity right from the start and especially for making things memorable. When I spend time with Tony, I feel like he's nurturing my mind. These kinds of friends are invaluable. I've always believed that when the student is ready, the teachers appear. Tony, John, and Bill were just a few of the many great teachers of my life thus far. I'm beyond grateful for everyone who has helped me become.

VIPs

✔ If you want real relationships that enrich your life, you must be real with others and especially with yourself.

✔ Seek to understand first and second to be understood.

✔ Learning to be unattached to the outcome allows you to make room for possibility.

✔ In most cases, your net worth mirrors the levels of your five closest friends. Who you spend your time with is who you become.

✔ It's up to you to protect your own energy and vision by being selective about who you choose to let into your inner circle.

CHAPTER 6
TRANSPARENCY

Cold-calling various large companies was something I had to do pretty regularly during the early stages of my career as a corporate trainer. I'm not a hunter, yet this process felt a lot like tracking down an animal, narrowing in, and executing at just the right time. I would spend hours trudging along the trail leading to the decision makers, chiseling away at each gatekeeper until I finally broke through. The uphill battle of cold-calling took so much of my energy, that by the time I received my first invite to train, I was completely mentally unprepared. My first thought was, "What the hell? How am I going to do this?" I had gotten what I wanted, but these were high-profile people, and my resume couldn't even get me into their cafeteria. Now it was completely up to me to go in, deliver value, and get results—I was terrified.

As you can imagine, time and experience helped me overcome my fears. Before speaking engagements, I used to blast the song "Thunderstruck" by AC/DC in my car. Singing at the top of my lungs and drumming on the steering wheel, I would enter a peak state of mind. I would also watch myself speak in the mirror, taking note of my tone of voice and facial expressions to better connect with my audience. Another strategy I used was to put twenty-five coins in my pocket, moving one from the left pocket to the right each time I interacted with someone. Despite my fears, I wouldn't let myself end the day until I had moved all the coins from the left pocket to the right. Although I don't get nervous quite as much as I used to anymore, I still get really excited about coaching or even simply speaking to powerful people. In my early days I would keep my nerves and excitement bottled up inside, whereas now I just tell my audience how I feel. Being transparent in these moments helps me own my emotions and keeps me humble as well. For years I had looked forward to being in a position where I could influence corporate authorities at the highest level. Sharing my gratitude in these moments reminds me of my beginnings, allowing me to appreciate my success even more.

I'm fortunate to be a part of a greater company that values transparency as much as I do. This morning I hosted a presentation and had the opportunity to express to everyone just how honored I am to be a part of one of the fastest-growing real estate companies in the world. I opened my presentation by sharing my backstory. I've discovered that sharing your adversities, failures, and challenges makes you immediately more relatable to people on their level. When all they know is your success, an audience is more likely to put you on a pedestal and put themselves in the pit. But if you talk about your vulnerabilities, insecurities, and fears, then people relate to you more easily. When you put all your cards on the table, you become more authentic and real.

When you put all your cards on the table, you become more authentic and real.

How transparent are you with yourself? It's tough to be transparent with others when you are not in tune with yourself. If you're not sure how to do this, a good place to start would be scheduling time for activities that are important to you – not for anyone else, just you. Think of things that bring you joy, self-expression, and fulfillment. Consider activities that you could do for hours and get lost in time. Many people are afraid to actually be alone with themselves because they're not at peace with who they are. They find comfort in the distractions of life and escaping from themselves rather than connecting with who they are. Others just don't have the time, patience, or courage to put in the work that this requires. It's easier for them to stay focused on their career, or even the affairs of other people rather than for themselves. My advice is to seek out self-help books or courses in training and development to invest in yourself. If you're not sure where to look, ask people you trust and respect their recommendations. If you want to change your life, *you've got to change your life*. To change your life, begin by changing your daily habits and your routines. What are your repetive patterns? Be open to discovering the reason behind why you do what you do each day or the way you respond to circumstances.

People who are disconnected from themselves often struggle to connect with people around them. The more we understand ourselves, the better we're able to help other people understand themselves and the world around them. Tatiana's experience as a retired high school teacher is a great example of this. While teaching French grammar, every now and again a student would ask a question that would leave her stumped. Instead of trying to cover up her blind spot and potentially mislead them, Tatiana would say, "I don't know," and call her mom in front of the class. Her mom was the perfect French teacher and a grammar wiz who was always willing to help. This approach not only allowed Tatiana to give her class a response with confidence, but the kids also loved the interaction with her mom. The entire room would fill with awe as they waited for her mom to answer. The students could more easily relate to Tatiana as having a mother, as not having every answer, and as being transparent enough to admit it. There are few people who, when put on the spot, have the courage to admit that they don't know something.

Transparency is a subset of integrity, in the sense that being transparent means upholding the truth. As a public speaker, a big part of my job is to keep an audience engaged and entertained. One of the challenges I face is balancing a tendency to embellish stories with a desire to uphold my integrity. I've been able to manage this by giving my audience warnings before stretching the truth. Besides that, if I'm going to brag, I'm going to be upfront about it. I'm also careful to ask for permission when borrowing someone else's story. People in my inner circle sometimes get annoyed when I ask for permission to embellish their anecdotes because they know I'm going to do it anyway. But it's better to have a reputation for being overly cautious than one for stepping on toes. I don't particularly enjoy bragging or talking about myself for long periods of time, so I preface by explaining the motivation behind sharing my success stories. Assuring an audience of my credibility is important because I believe in only taking advice from people who have already accomplished the goals you are looking to reach.

Recently, I've been particularly mindful of balancing transparency with humility. I've been working on accepting compliments without adding too much information unless further asked. Several people have noticed that I have recently released a lot of weight, and I've been receiving more compliments than usual. In the past, I would have overlooked social cues and immediately started describing my health journey in enormous detail. To avoid potentially being boastful, I now make a conscious effort to simply accept the compliment with a thank-you, remembering that less is more. Only when people engage me by asking specific questions, do I presume they're truly interested in learning more.

When I do share personal stories, it's because I've learned that it can be valuable for people to know your struggles, so their own process is

Being transparent means upholding the truth.

more relatable. Being open about my mistakes and failures makes my lessons more believable, and in turn, makes me a more effective public speaker. Again, it's about moving away from the pedestal and presenting myself in a way that allows people see *themselves* in me. Keep in mind that it takes courage to look within and acknowledge your own flaws. Society's obsession with image has grown to unattainable levels, which means fewer and fewer people are willing to admit imperfection. But society does not define you or me. The reality is that mistakes and imperfections are a part of life. There is value in imperfection. Have you ever considered that flaws and mistakes can actually be gifts? I've come to believe that there are no mistakes, only lessons. Step one is to accept this reality. Step two is to be transparent about your shortcomings so that you may grow from them.

I challenge you to take it a step further, be vulnerable and share your mistakes with other people. Even though I have achieved success, I still look to others for guidance and inspiration. One of the ways I continue to change and evolve is by learning from the experience of those around me. Other people's stories often remind me of my own journey, and these moments can be very emotional for me. I've been known to cry while watching *American Idol* contestants open up about their insecurities and self-esteem issues because I see my former self in them. Seeing people on the brink of a major breakthrough is overwhelming for me, but I embrace these experiences because they remind me to continue working on myself. My growth is not limited. Awareness and transparency are lifetime commitments.

In 1995, I was asked to speak to Investors Group Financial Services. The region manager, Perry Catena, invited me to give a speech at an event held at a golf course in Canada. I was still a student at Toastmasters, and truth be told, I was terrified. After the training, they handed out "schwag bags," with golf shirts, hats, t-shirts, and a few other items. When I got home that night, I noticed an envelope in my bag. I opened it and found a fifty-dollar honorarium tucked in a thank-you card from the company. It was a very powerful moment in my life because up until then, I had never been paid to speak. This turning point is when I realized, "Wow! I can actually get paid to do what I love to do." To be fully transparent, I truly didn't think my skills were worthy of payment at the time. That unexpected gift taught me that the value and knowledge I'm capable of bringing to an audience has real value. Since then, I've charged much larger amounts for my keynote services, but I still cherish those fifty dollars. It wasn't something I had negotiated; it was simply a token of appreciation that helped me recognize my worth.

That being said, I think much of my success truly boils down to the way I approach relationships—an approach that emphasizes the importance of being transparent. When I meet new people, I tend to open up quickly, sharing facts about myself in order to help them feel comfortable in opening up as well. This transparent sharing is often my first shot at building relationship equity. We've all heard the saying, "Fake it till you make it." I don't judge people for abiding by these words, yet life has taught me to err on the side of caution, especially when I'm around other successful people who have lots of history and experience. These people are typically very in tune and can easily tell when someone is faking it. It's better to just be real and transparent because it's a safer, more sustainable approach.

When you're a nobody in a sea of accomplished people, it's easy to hide behind others. Reaching higher levels begets greater visibility and exposure. Never assume you are not being observed. The intensity of this observation grows in correlation with your success. About ten years ago, I was approached by a network marketing health company. I agreed to meet with the co-founders of the company to discuss their new car qualifier program. They were running a BMW promotion in which top performers were rewarded with a lease for a cool new car. I was then offered a deal that involved me personally paying for a car lease, and using my own social media accounts to create a buzz around their promotion. The men explained that once I generated enough activity and recruitment, the company would take over the financial obligation of the lease, and I would walk away with a free BMW. I did not move forward with this because there was misleading marketing information that was not in integrity.

The network marketing space has come a long way since then. Selling the dream is still part of the approach, yet the dream is not as overembellished as it was years ago. On the other hand, social media has become a complex monster of an issue. There is no shortage of people who love to show off private jets, pretty girls, private islands, and super cars—none of which they actually own. And there's no shortage of people who are fooled into thinking that these people deserve their likes, follows, comments, and attention. I walked away from the BMW deal because it lacked integrity. I encourage you to walk away from anything that lacks integrity. As I said before, being transparent means upholding the truth.

There are people who are able to pass under false pretenses for months or even years. "Time will either promote you or expose you— it's just a matter of time." If you continually lie to others, a day will come when people realize it. If you lie to yourself about your health, it's bound to catch up to you soon. If you try to convince yourself that your marriage isn't that bad, you're going to wake up one day and realize the biggest mistake was not choosing the wrong spouse; rather, it was lying to yourself for so long. Telling the truth takes courage because it sucks to look bad or flawed, but it's better to do it now than ten years from now. Heal a wound now before it turns into a full-blown disease.

My journey has been challenging, and I've been tested in monumental ways. I reached a rock-bottom level that's lower than most people have experienced, yet, in a strange way I consider it a blessing because I came out tougher. My skin is thick, which means criticism and rejection don't devastate me like they once did. I welcome and encourage people to help me uncover my blind spots in order for me to have a more influential life. Yet, I'm still a person and I have fears just like everyone else. Thinking about the sheer growth of the real estate company I serve on, and the 100,000-plus agents, sends a jolt of insecurity throughout my body. The critical voice inside my head pipes up and tells me I'm not good enough to support such a massive effort.

From a young age I knew I was different—an odd ball. My classmates would avoid me, and I would always be picked last for teams in gym class. I would worry about spending too much time with people because seeing who I really was might have made them uncomfortable. To make things worse, I spent over twenty-five years traveling to different cities every other day. It's impossible to build deep connections with people when you've always got a plane to catch—so I just didn't do

Time will either promote you or expose you—it's just a matter of time.

it. Surprising as it may sound, this fear of getting truly close to people is something I continue to battle each day. I am continuously in the process of being mindful to talk *with* people instead of only talking *to* people. It's more natural for people to only talk about topics that are comfortable or safe. The closer you let someone get to you, the deeper your connection, and the more potential they have to hurt you. This fear of vulnerability and loss of control can be terrifying and needs daily practice and attention in order to overcome.

To this day, I struggle with the idea that I'm unlovable. Experience has taught me that staying intentional about my mindset and surroundings can off-set the inner critic. We all have an inner critical voice—it's the condition of being human that will never go away. You need to seek ways to discover how to manage your self-doubt. Not every day is going to be positive. You're not going to be happy every moment. It's a daily, constant, and reoccurring decision to choose how you are going to respond. Are you going to let the inner critic take you out of the game? Each day I stay aware of my environment, both physically and mentally, so I can determine if a threat is real or if I'm just scared. If you saw a long shape up ahead on a hiking trail, you might be startled at first. But after a few moments you'd ask yourself, "Is it is a snake or a twig?" The things we fear in life often present no real danger. The fear is real, but the threat is not. We need to be mindful of this reality otherwise, our self-limiting thoughts come right back.

I'm not sure what your personal journey looks like, though I am sure you've also been tested. You have your own fears, problems, demons, and critical voice. I know this because you and I are *human*, and our journeys are much like moving targets. We should all strive to be better than the persons we were yesterday; however, we need to remember that none of us are perfect. There's no point in pretending to be.

VIPs

- ✔ It's tough to be transparent with others when you are not in tune with yourself. The more you understand yourself, the better you're able to help other people understand themselves and the world around them.

- ✔ Be transparent about your shortcomings so that you may grow from them.

- ✔ When you're a nobody in a sea of accomplished people, it's easy to hide behind others. Reaching higher levels begets greater visibility and exposure.

- ✔ None of us are perfect, so there's no point in pretending to be.

CHAPTER 7
COLLABORATION

Back in the nineties, I had the privilege of attending Toastmasters. During the first night of our meeting, all the guests were asked to take turns standing up and introducing themselves. By the time there were three people ahead of me, my legs were shaking violently underneath the table. When I stood up for my turn, I was so terrified that I completely forgot who I was and had to look down at my name tag to figure it out. Shortly after, we were asked to prepare and present a three-to-five-minute speech about ourselves for the "Icebreaker" event later that week. Our speeches would be evaluated by a panel of four people, including the "Sergeant-at-Arms" who was in charge of reporting the "ums" and "aahs" of each presenter. Throughout the days leading up to this event, I spent many hours practicing in front of a mirror. My nights were spent tossing and turning in bed, thinking about the impossible task ahead of me.

After several sleepless nights, the "Icebreaker" event had finally arrived. I did my best to hide my profuse sweating and general terror, but I was clearly a wreck. Following the first session of speeches, we were given a fifteen-minute break before starting up again. Can you guess whose name was first in line for the second session? At the beginning of the break, I ran to the nearest hotel washroom and threw up in the sink. Looking up at myself in the mirror, I thought, "I physically can't do this." With only ten minutes left, I knew I had to think fast and buy myself some time. Making a personal excuse would be too obvious a lie, which meant I had to find a way to postpone the entire session.

It's illegal to pull a false fire alarm in most countries. Yet, desperate times call for desperate measures. I began weighing out what the scenario would look like if someone were to catch me. Would I end up with a criminal record? Would the charge be a misdemeanor? Would I spend the rest of Toastmasters sitting in a jail cell? I pictured the entire hotel having to evacuate because I was too nervous to talk about myself for a few minutes. After carefully considering the pros and cons, I decided the worst-case scenario was that I would just end up paying a fine. When no one was looking, I slipped into a hallway and pulled the alarm. Nothing. *The alarm didn't work!* No sound. No evacuation. No fire department. As it turns out, the hotel was equipped with an internal alarm system for non-emergencies that, when triggered, would alert the hotel front desk with a flashing light. The staff quickly realized it was a false alarm, and a maintenance man was sent to reset the system. I managed to postpone the session for zero additional minutes. Toastmasters–1, Darren–0.

When I say I've had to overcome a lot to get to where I am today, I truly mean it. My fear of speaking to strangers—especially groups of them—held me back for many years. I think the biggest challenge this presented was that it made it impossible for me to have a balanced set of values. It's more difficult to understand the importance of collaboration when you have a crippling fear of the steps that lead toward collaboration. For years, I would avoid situations that I consider to be extremely valuable today, situations that could have very likely opened doors for me at a younger age. Sometimes I wish I had gone to Toastmasters sooner in life, but in reality, I probably wasn't ready for the experience. I try not to think about what I would have done to the hotel if my desperation prior to the "Icebreaker" had been heightened any further.

My younger self couldn't even imagine many of the thoughts, beliefs, and values I currently have today. We are entirely different people. Thinking about this past version of myself makes me appreciate the work that went into building the mindset and life I have today. At present, collaboration is something that I cannot live without. This value is deeply intertwined with the way I approach my work, relationships, social life, and more. Since I was a child, I've always been deeply curious about how people do what they do. Today the difference is that I'm no longer afraid to connect with other people and figure it out. I've learned that collaboration often begins with learning small facts and details about someone, such as their daily habits, interests, goals, and hobbies. I mentioned before that the contact cards in my phone are full of thorough notes with details such as these because they create starting points for collaboration. You never know who might become a partner, ally, confidant, helper, or friend down the line.

Even the success of my humanitarian trips relies heavily on collaboration. I look to my network of friends and colleagues for advice regarding safety, cultural differences, best time of year to travel, best places to stay, and even people to meet. Travelling for pleasure often leads to great opportunities for me to meet with potential clients, so I like reaching out to connections at my destinations. Although I'm technically doing work, it doesn't feel that way because I love what I do. I love stepping into the vast network of conversations and facilitating collaboration among some of the world's top achievers. And as crazy as it is to say—I've become the kind of person who loves collaborating with complete strangers too.

At present, collaboration is something that I cannot live without.

Years ago, while walking to a lunch meeting downtown, I passed a homeless man with a sign in front of the Vancouver Convention Center. He was asking passersby for spare change. I stopped and asked him how much money he was looking for. "I just need twenty-five dollars to get into the hostel. I want to stay there tonight," he replied. This man piqued my interest, so I continued asking him questions. "How are you today? Are a lot of people walking by? Are they actually giving you money?" The guy told me most people kept walking, and those who stopped gave him less than a dollar. I decided to offer him a deal. "If you ask every person that walks by for a hundred dollars, I'll come back and buy you a meal after my meeting." He stared back at me with bug eyes, telling me I was crazy. "Whatever you lack in skill, you make up in numbers. I want you to change your ask so that you change your results," I said.

The guy was pretty perplexed when I walked away, yet I had a good feeling about the situation. An hour and a half later, I headed back to the convention center again. In the distance, I saw a shaggy head of hair spring up from the crowd on the sidewalk. The man hurried toward me with excitement and good news written all over his face. "Hey mister!" he shouted. "You wouldn't believe what happened!" He came to me with outstretched arms, ready to give me a giant hug. The poor guy hadn't showered in a while, so I did my best to dodge it. Winded and ecstatic, he explained that he was able to collect a whopping $76.20. "One guy told me I had big balls asking for a hundred dollars, so he gave me a twenty! Lots of people gave me fives and tens too!" he said smiling. In honor of our deal, I bought him a meal, wished him well, and went about my day.

My hope is that the lesson I was able to share with the homeless man continued to serve him long after we parted ways. This story also demonstrates the important point that there is often an element of service to practicing collaboration. Working with someone, or a larger group of people, to achieve a common goal typically means giving up a piece of yourself to make things happen. As I say this, I can't help but to think of Glenn Sanford, a dear friend and the founder of eXp World

When you change your ask, you change your results.

Holdings, Inc. (NASDAQ: EXPI). During the last summer before the COVID pandemic, I attended a meeting in Bellingham, Washington, alongside 200 of the most influential agents, leaders, and collaborators associated with our company. Glenn was given the tough job of announcing compensation changes to the entire team that day. As usual, the phrase "compensation changes" sent a little shockwave of whispers and murmurs throughout the audience. Glenn stayed perfectly calm and cool as he spoke to the audience and said, "It's not me who's deciding. We are deciding this together." Glenn believes in and embodies collaboration, which is one of the many reasons he is the caliber of leader I strive to be.

There are many small changes and adjustments a leader can make to be more collaborative, as well as encourage this value throughout their team. During seminars, it's a good practice to seat the audience at round tables rather than theater or classroom style. I have found this to be a more effective use of everyone's time and space, especially if there are attendees from multiple companies or industries. When people are forced to face each other, they're far more likely to meet, connect, and enhance each other's individual experiences. Round tables create equality and spark creativity. If you can, mix the groups according to personality differences, history, and experience. Also, always provide food and beverages—even if it has to come out of your own budget. People worldwide use food as a way to relax, socialize, and naturally connect with one another. It also gives people something to do with their hands, which is always a good thing.

As a corporate trainer, I often come across executives and leaders who struggle to leave their secluded offices. Leaders who wish to be well rounded and involved must find ways to step outside and invest time working alongside the front lines, in the trenches. It's crucial to connect and collaborate with the people running the factories, the brick-and-mortar locations, and filling the critical customer-facing positions. The carrier service UPS is a great example of collaboration within their corporate hierarchy. The board of directors always includes one or two real delivery drivers because UPS values communication and synergy down the line. At eXp, we have a licensed agent who sits on our board of directors as well. We also have an entire agent advisory council to facilitate communication among all levels of the company. If you happen to be a leader of a team or company, be sure to connect with as many people in your organization as possible.

Another small adjustment a leader can make to create a more collaborative work environment is to reframe the thoughts and mindsets of team members toward the value of collaboration. When I was young and just beginning to chip away at my social fears, my understanding of collaboration was relatively superficial. Once my fears subsided and I was able to gain real-time experience, it became clear that collaboration is a powerful tool—one that can only serve you if you're willing to be open with others. When a problem presents itself, you can only go as far as your mind allows you to go, that is, unless you're able to reach out into the world and ask for help. In order to be successful, businesses and their leaders have to continually get better at problem solving. In my experience, the first step is to get better at collaborating.

Maybe you're wondering where to begin. My answer is *anywhere and everywhere*. There is rarely a time when I don't engage people in conversation. This past summer, I was swimming in the Pacific Ocean and hit it off with a guy who happened to be floating near me. We ended up talking about his goals as a software engineer and continued chatting for a few minutes. A couple of weeks later, we decided to have lunch to discuss a possible investment opportunity. Another time, while at the Opal Sands Resort in Clearwater Beach, Florida, I started thinking about possibly getting my own United States Investor Visa. I was relaxing in the hot tub, alone, until another man popped in. We struck up a conversation, and I quickly discovered that he was an immigration attorney who had specific experience working with Canadians—freaking awesome.

Many people go to hot tubs to relax, but I see hot tubs as an opportunity zone. Those who know me best have said, "There isn't a time when Darren doesn't talk. He *never* doesn't talk." Others jokingly say they get exhausted just by watching me do my thing, yet I thrive from it. Now that I've conquered my insecurities and fears, collaboration isn't work—it's play. Simple as it is, it feels good to be good at what I do. I think one of the big reasons people are willing to talk and collaborate with me is because I don't have a hidden agenda. I'm curious, I ask questions, and genuinely want to know more. My intentions are rooted in that same curiosity I've had since I was a child. In my experience, this quality makes me more memorable. Yes, this may sound cheesy to you, but I'll say it anyway. I'm incredibly fortunate to have experienced many of the hardships I went through. As tough as it was for me to mature and evolve, I'm grateful my life unfolded the way it did.

Moving forward, I encourage you to get curious about people, to ask questions more often than you're probably used to—follow the eighty-twenty rule—and to simply get out of your head. Life doesn't happen inside of our minds; it happens when we interact with our surroundings and especially with other people. Sometimes we try collaborating with the voice inside our head for too long, leading to something I call *analysis paralysis*. It's easy to get trapped in this state, so my prescription is to go out and talk to people who can provide you with great feedback, insights, open doors, and possibly even more connections.

We are all on separate paths that are uniquely distinct from one another in infinite ways. It can be easy to judge ourselves, and our process, especially in comparison to those succeeding around us. Keep in mind that society tends to broadcast success more often than backstory. We see glitter and gold more than we see sweat and struggle. For some, the path is relatively short and painless. For others, it's grueling, long, and perhaps forces them to backtrack before progressing again. We can't assume to know what a person went through to reach success, so we shouldn't compare our paths against theirs. My path was extremely long and definitely tough, yet I knew in my heart that I would eventually become. Thus, I continued fighting. Now that I've come out on the other side, I'm beyond grateful I did.

VIPs

- ✔ The world is a giant network of conversations; all you have to do is step into it.

- ✔ There is often an element of service to practicing collaboration. Working with someone, or a larger group of people, to achieve a common goal typically means giving up a piece of yourself to make things happen.

- ✔ When you have the right mindset, collaboration becomes a powerful problem-solving tool.

- ✔ If you happen to be a leader of a team or company, be sure to step outside of the office and connect with as many people in your organization as possible.

- ✔ Talking to the voice inside your head for too long can lead to *analysis paralysis*. Get out of your head and connect with others to make the most of life.

Pictured with the master Bob Proctor; a man who has shared multiple words of wisdom and greatly impacted Darren's mindset

A meeting several years ago with one of the most profound writers—Mark Victor Hansen is a co-author behind *Chicken Soup for the Soul* Series

"Being down and out doesn't mean you're down and out. I was up and out."

"A trip with purpose can change your life."

Darren in one of his favorite homes in which he lived throughout a seven month lease term

LY2NK Foundation was the result of a life-changing 2018 trip to Liberia, West Africa with *Awakening Giants*.

CHAPTER 8

TENACITY

Each of the values I've shared so far has played a significant role in my personal path to success. Among the hundreds of values that exist in our world, I'm confident there are some that align more closely with your individual path. I hope you're able to invest time in exploring them, as well as their impact, through your choices in life. That being said, I sincerely believe, in addition to perseverance, tenacity is fundamental to every success story—past, present, and future. A person's ability to complete meaningful work is defined by their commitment to their commitments. Most people are capable of dreaming, yet it's been said that only three percent of the world's population consciously set any goals at all. Most can express their desires and plans for the future, yet few people succeed at following through over sustained periods of time. The people who fall within the three percent who actually embrace tenacity accomplish more than the other ninety-seven percent combined.

It's easier to carry on when a process or undertaking is going well and when things are running smoothly. Unfortunately, discomfort and challenges often put a swift end to people's action and determination. Part of the problem is that people tend to place too much focus on functional goals, such as starting a new business, landing the next promotion, or reaching foreign markets. I have found that it's equally important to focus on the short and long-term effects of achieving that goal. Try asking yourself, "How will my life look different once I reach my target?" When we allow ourselves to stay focused on the pursuit of a better lifestyle, then we are more likely to stay motivated. Many of the decisions I make on a day-to-day basis are simple. I just take a pause and ask myself, "Will this bring me more freedom or less freedom?" If the answer is more, then I continue the work until it's finished because I know it will lead to an overall better life.

After presentations and speaking events, people often approach me wanting to know the specifics of how I was able to build my corporate training team. They share dreams of traveling the globe and speaking at world-famous stages just as I had many years ago. Typically, I see people's energy shift dramatically when I explain that I was only able to build my corporate training team after practicing in front of mirrors for hours every single day and by making 400 daily cold calls for several years. I've seen people completely rethink their lives right in front of me while envisioning themselves having to put in all the behind-the-scenes work. People chase after a lifestyle, yet they're not committed to making the necessary moves to get there. My life changed when I stopped making announcements, started taking action, and began earning my experience through hard work. Most people *do* put in effort; however, effort doesn't outperform real experience.

Effort doesn't outperform real experience.

Like any normal person, I'm lazy when it comes to doing things I genuinely don't like to do. For example, I'd much rather leave cleaning and cooking up to someone else. Now that I've invested in a lifestyle where I don't have to worry about these activities, I have the freedom to dedicate more time to business and finance—two things I'm able to hyper-focus on with pure enjoyment. I don't procrastinate when it comes to revenue-generating activities because I don't need external motivation or inspiration to do them. I happily work for assets, because working for money doesn't sustain the lifestyle I desire. It's about having so much income that you don't need a budget. It's about using your assets to pay for your lifestyle—not just your money.

Again, it's freedom that drives me the most in life. Ask yourself what you really want, more than anything else, from this gift of life. Write it down. Next, make a list of the five most important things you're committed to in your life. Then ask the following critical thinking questions: Do my commitments align with what I want most? Are my habits, actions, and behaviors congruent with my commitments? I have always envisioned a global life. My dream started coming true the minute I decided to change the details of my days to align with my vision.

Much of what I've said in this book probably appeals to the logic-oriented section of your mind. "Darren, could it really be that simple?" In theory, the answer is yes. Nevertheless, we are complex humans, with complex lives, and we're constantly being bombarded with complex problems. It's unrealistic to think we can be tenacious every waking moment. When I find myself falling off track and losing momentum, I turn to my role models. As a teenager, I worked as a maintenance man cleaning the swimming pool and cutting the grass for a motel, called The Swift Motel, in Swift Current, Saskatchewan. All throughout my employment, a man named Joe Arling was the proud owner and operator of this small business. Over the years, the closer I got to Joe, the fonder I grew of him. I learned so much by simply observing him at work, especially the way he treated customers.

One weekend, two celebrities from the TV show *Dallas* arrived in a black SUV. They checked into the motel in the hopes of doing a little Canadian goose hunting. I was on the Harley Davidson golf cart, taking them and their luggage to their room, when it occurred to me that I was driving the stars I watched on television. Proximity is power, whether it's political, financial, celebrity, academic, or educational power. Joe knew this. Even in a town of less than 20,000 people, he was able to attract TV celebrities to a small motel. Joe was always networking, gaining corporate accounts, and winning business. He taught me how to be curious about how I could get in proximity of people in positions of power. For how tenacious Joe was about getting customers, he was even more so about keeping them. Through conversations and making requests, he would have guests booking their next stay before they left. Even to this day, very few small businesses I frequent practice this level of customer retention.

It's been over thirty years since I've seen Joe, but I still have flashbacks of my time with him. When I'm lacking motivation to see something through, these memories urge me to stay committed. If you really want to live out tenacity, then think of the people in your own life who double down on the follow-through. Remember the people who put x's in all the boxes and who keep going when things get tough. These are going to be your role models. If you haven't already done so, I encourage you to make memories with these people. Treasure these moments and allow them to fuel your mindset. Concentrating on your role models can enable you to feed your focus and starve your distractions—a sure path to success.

My childhood neighbor is another one of my tenacious role models. She is a former deputy premier of Saskatchewan who worked under Premiere Grant Devine in the mid-eighties. I've mentioned Pat Smith before, and I don't hesitate to praise her again. Before meeting her, I was a very insecure kid who didn't even have the nerve to approach neighbors or other people in my community. I watched and studied people, but I was far too scared to get to know them. Pat showed me enough kindness to slowly help me overcome the mental barriers I would place between myself and others. I quickly grew comfortable around her and came to learn that Pat was a tenacious firecracker. As a woman of power and influence, she often fell under criticism simply because she was a public figure. She was frequently attacked for defending the things she stood for, yet this never stopped her from building relationships with people. Despite falling into the line of fire, over and over again, she continued to have faith and optimism toward strangers. She gave everyone the benefit of the doubt—including me.

If it weren't for Pat, I would likely be a very different person today. She planted the seed of tenacity in me at a young age. It may have taken years for this quality to fully blossom within me, yet I recognize and honor where it came from. I was just a kid back then, and little did I know that my moments with Pat would go on to shape my adult career. Her gift to me was one of the big reasons why I was able to continue knocking on big corporate doors, even after years of hearing "no." One failed phone call after another, I kept going because she taught me to do so. I was taught to keep calling—and in the early days, to keep physically knocking. Pat is one of the biggest reasons why I followed up with a company for seventeen years before getting a "yes." Thank you, Pat Smith, for being one of the great tenacious role models of my life.

Recently, I was introduced to a gentleman who further expanded my understanding of what it means to have tenacity. For years, I moved through life with the mentality that tenacious people made big, loud moves. Tony Jeary introduced me to a Texan billionaire who is on my must meet list. This billionaire is my image of tenacity—people who consistently work through to completion, making things happen on a major scale as a low-profile person with high impact. This gentleman taught me that you don't necessarily need to have a high profile to make a high impact. While in Dallas on other business, we decided to meet up to chat about business and life. The objective of his company is to pool together capital and then strategically invest in promising companies. His work ethic is incredible. He hires brilliant people to work for him while steering clear from getting involved in the operations of selected companies. He raises big checks, but he prefers to stay behind the scenes, working strictly as an investor. I knew he was a very wealthy man; however, I didn't realize how few people knew this fact. My friend's discipline, focus, and ability to persevere resulted in massive payoff. In business, you either make money or you lose money. He chooses to make it. Thanks to our friendship, I have a greater appreciation for tenacious people like him.

There are many reasons why people become successful. Some begin their process with a jump start; others begin with a handicap. Some begin blissfully ignorant and with few worries; others begin timidly out of fear for losing what's at stake. Your history is unique; therefore, the specific set of challenges you face will also be uniquely yours. However, it's very likely that many of your individual challenges have been experienced by others before you. This is why I encourage everyone to seek out tenacious role models and get advice from mentors who have done whatever it is you hope to accomplish. Also, study your own habits and tendencies so that you can better focus on *high leverage activities.* Tony uses this term to help his clients identify the activities that allow them to reach their goals more quickly and efficiently. These activities support a person's overall values and directly affect where they are now, versus where they want to be. Tenacity alone holds little value. Tenacity combined with a clear direction and a strong ability to focus leads to wins. We all have twenty-four-hour days. The problem is lack of direction, not lack of time. My personal experience in the early days is a testament to this truth.

As a young, relatively inexperienced small business owner, I not only managed the entire operation, I also did virtually everything else as well. It was impossible for me to get ahead financially, and I soon discovered that my heavy involvement was actually hurting both my personal and business success. I was exhausting my energy reserves on low leverage— or minimum wage activities—which made it impossible for me to grow. Another mentor approached me, explaining that it was time for me to refocus my attention and double down on activities that would lead to higher returns. We spoke specifically about my traveling and habits surrounding this activity. He pointed out that I was wasting time by looking for the best hotel, flight, and rental car deals. This was a poor

The problem is lack of direction, not lack of time.

use of my energy because it didn't result in increased profits. Since then, I have learned to outsource these types of tasks by hiring travel agents or assistants to organize them for me. This major change in my approach to business has allowed me to pour more of my energies into the activities that grant me the ability to commit myself to a life of significance.

This period of growth resulted in many changes in my life, my approach to work, and my views. For starters, I realized that life isn't happening to me; it's happening for me. Rather than letting life affect me as a passive bystander, I learned that I could design a life in such a way that it would fulfill me with greater happiness. It's not just the dream—it's how it makes you feel and how it validates you. Your hard work should give you positive feelings of accomplishment. I also realized that your identifiable high-leverage activities ought to align with your values *as well as* your innate gifts. I recognize that there are men and women who truly enjoy doing many of the activities that I consider to be low leverage. Even though it's the bane of my existence, lots of people gain inner peace or validation from cooking. And there are plenty of people who procrastinate when it comes to business or finance-based activities because these don't align with their list of values. This is precisely why it's so important to be in tune with yourself—so that you're able to see the patterns in your own behavioral tendencies and relentlessly chase after the goals that fit within your definition of success.

Identifiable high-leverage activities ought to align with your values *as well as* your innate gifts.

I'd like to discuss an important subset of tenacity—sustainability. Sustainable efforts can lead to ripples of impact that carry on for generations. Some of the greats such as Jim Rohn and Zig Ziglar are prime examples of tenacious, accomplished people whose words and actions will serve as reminders all over the world of their legacy for years to come. It's noble to pursue sustainable achievement as these distinguished men have. It's also critical for long-term success. All of your choices, actions, and decisions will build upon each another, so you must consider sustainability along the way. As you continue to design your life and career, I encourage you to remain cautious with each step you take. No matter how big or small, be sure your moves lead to continued growth.

Also, be sure to stay mindful of your daily routines. I've experienced trying days in which my daily habits and routines were the only thing that gave me enough motivation to push through. You're not going to feel good every day. Some days, you won't feel inspired in the slightest way. I think of motivation as a warm bath—it has a limited shelf-life; therefore, we must find other ways to stay inspired. Daily routines are one of the ways I supplement motivation. In my early days, every now and again, I used to lose the confidence and drive needed to go out and sell my corporate training services. Instead of letting a day slip by unproductively, I would carry on with my routine, forcing myself to go out and meet people regardless.

Similarly, stepping into a chamber of commerce or networking event sometimes made me feel insecure. I'd compare myself to all the successful people around me and minimize myself to the point where I didn't feel like I could contribute. Despite this inner turmoil, I'd stick to the plan and mingle, knowing that I was still capable of generating activity simply based on the law of averages. I'll repeat it again— whatever you lack in skill, you make up in numbers. My mornings are yet another example of how I use routines to create sustained tenacity in my life. Some of my morning routines include thanking every part of my body, thanking the universe for the ability to open my eyes and live another day, experiencing gratitude before getting out of bed, taking a cold shower, reading my goals, writing out my goals, and journaling. I'm a firm believer that if you win the morning, you win the day.

I'd like to close this chapter by pointing out that the source of my motivation has shifted within the past few years. I have a strong and deep desire to continually level up, and I'm guessing this will likely never change. My desire to build more net worth, however, is now rooted in global philanthropy. A couple of years ago, I met a guy who asked me how I was doing financially. At the time, I was doing pretty well and told him so. Then he asked, "Are you able to write a check to a children's hospital for a million dollars and carry on with your current lifestyle?" The question rattled my brain. After collecting my thoughts, I replied, explaining that I couldn't. "You're broke then," he replied. He told me to return in a few years, once I've successfully donated the sum of money with the same caveat.

This conversation caused me to completely rethink my motives entirely, as well as my long-term goals. I've always been the kind of person to respond very emotionally to suffering in the world. Acts of service is my love language, so it would only make sense for me to have an innate desire to help people in need. And yet, it admittedly took me a little while to embrace my love language as a motivation for increasing my net worth. Earlier I mentioned that I am committed to a life of significance. My definition of significance has grown and evolved considerably within the past few years. My goal is to stay mentally tough until I'm able to give back to my heart's content—until I become the ultimate giver.

VIPs

✔ Tenacity is fundamental to every success story—past, present, and future.

✔ I make decisions based on whether a result will bring me more freedom or less freedom.

✔ My life changed when I stopped making announcements, started taking action, and began earning experience through hard work.

✔ It's about using your assets to pay for your lifestyle—not just your money.

✔ Tenacity alone holds little value. Tenacity combined with a clear direction and a strong ability to focus leads to wins.

✔ Life isn't happening to you; it's happening for you.

Cleo, the little white dog with the chocolate brown nose. Tatiana and Darren's little Bichon-Shih Tzu has taught them more about love, compassion, and patience than anyone else

"Change your view and get a different perspective of life."

Visiting Squamish, B.C.

"Capture the sunset to create magical moments with your loved ones."

Trip to California to meet with Awakening Giants—the catalyst for LY2NK Foundation.

"Get out of your comfort zone and dance like nobody's watching."

Darren and Tatiana get to experience different cultures around the world.

CHAPTER 9
CLOSING THOUGHTS

Perseverance has been a consistent theme throughout my uphill journey, which is how we've landed on the title, *Until I Become.* I'm living proof that perseverance does pay off. That being said, reaching financial freedom is not my ultimate goal in life. When it comes to money, there are infinite levels of success. Once you reach a significant financial goal for the first time, it's often surprising to realize how the finish line has suddenly crept forward. I have not reached any form of success ceiling. As long as I'm alive, this journey will continue. My ultimate goal in life is to continue growing and becoming each and every day. In practice, this simply means morphing into a better version of the person I was yesterday, every day. If I set my mind on a goal, the competitive part of me takes over, and I usually don't find it hard to stay on track. At the same time though, I have to be careful not to compare my journey to the success of others around me.

Allowing comparison to feed my competitive instincts has resulted in much of my unhappiness in life. Experience and time have taught me that there's always going to be someone whose achievements make you feel like you're not doing enough. When I find myself looking to others as a gauge of my own success, I remind myself of a powerful lesson I learned a long time ago: It's not about the target; rather, it's all about who you become in the process of reaching that target. Though I know that I'm far from perfect and remain committed to furthering my growth, I'm proud of the person I have become

In the near future, my intention is to raise one hundred million dollars toward global philanthropy. I plan on travelling to 150 countries around the planet and stepping foot on all seven continents. I'm also currently concentrating on reaching the best physical shape of my life, and each day I work on having an extraordinary personal relationship with my life partner, Tatiana. Financially, my focus is to keep a stable and consistent portfolio of income-producing assets. My newest undertaking is to buy, build, and sell companies through mergers and acquisitions. After achieving these goals, I will not be the same person I am today, and I can't begin to explain how much the thought of this excites me.

Wherever you are in life, I'd like to challenge you to think about you dreams, goals, and vision. Consider the quality of person you'll become once you put your plan in action. Afterward, ask yourself whether this version of you reaches your absolute highest potential. Can you dream up an even better version of yourself? Remember that there are no ceilings to success in this world. The only limits are the ones we place on ourselves. Dream it, do it, become it.

Challenge Questions

Here are fourteen questions I'd like for you to ask yourself. These questions are designed to encourage self-reflection, to help clarify your overall objectives in life, and to help you identify room for improvement. I've provided my own responses to each question to stimulate ideas in case you find yourself needing direction.

1. **What steps have you taken to continue growing throughout your career journey into leadership?** I'm a firm believer that people stop growing when they stay comfortable for too long. The key to being a good leader is getting comfortable with being uncomfortable. In an effort to stay sharp, I've pushed myself to take on various challenges centered on a different theme each year. This year, for example, I've chosen to focus on mergers and acquisitions. I've always had an interest in the subject but never dedicated myself to exploring it more deeply. As I gain knowledge, I've discovered it's easier to *acquire* revenue than to *create* revenue. *When it comes to achieving most high-level goals, your deliberate action is*

often not required. Rather, it's all about creating powerful teams and powerful teamwork. Once in a position of leadership, your roles and responsibilities will likely change. It also becomes necessary for you to have foundational knowledge and understanding. However, you must have the ability to transfer the knowledge to someone else in a way that they can then apply it in practice. My mindset has expanded from simply having a vision on an individual level to creating a global vision through teams.

2. **What did your proudest and darkest moments teach you?** I think most of us remember individual moments more clearly than we do entire days. I embrace this pattern and have learned to make detailed records of life's most important moments by taking lots of pictures, jotting down interesting quotes and thoughts, and sharing inspirational messages via social media.

   My proudest moment taught me humility and perseverance. I learned to focus on daily habits and routines instead of relying on motivation. We've all experienced the urge to give up. In order to overcome this, I've learned that it's vital to practice discipline and follow through personal best practices and routines. Have a road map and a strategic plan in place so you don't feel lost, even when you feel unmotivated. It's also necessary to overcome self-doubt and any negative mind chatter or internal dialogue. If you let it win, you will undoubtedly fall into self-sabotage.

   Through my darkest moment, I learned how to protect money and multiply it. When my very survival was at stake, I released the notion that someone was coming to my rescue and accepted that it was entirely up to me to change my situation. Another huge takeaway from this experience was gratitude. I learned to be grateful for every moment because there is always someone out there in a situation far worse. You think your life is extraordinarily difficult but compared to what? It's all a matter of perception.

3. **What piece of advice do you wish you had when you were younger?** Anything you want or need in your life is going to come from people beyond yourself. The things you want will come to you

Darren Jacklin's Must Meet List

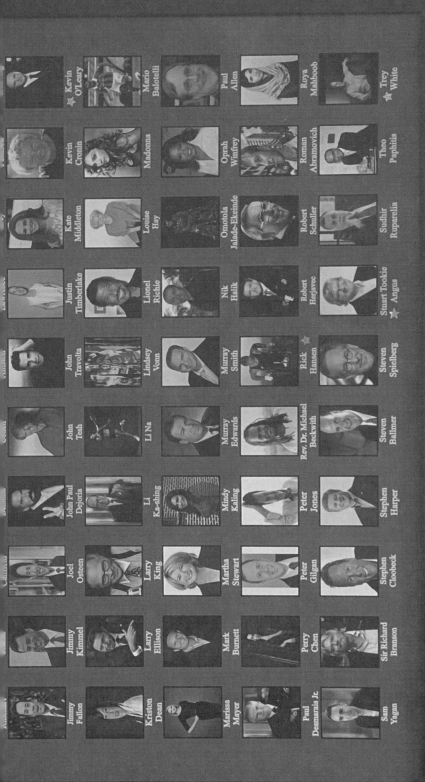

if you learn how to make powerful requests from other people. As human beings, we are all in a network of conversations. I mentioned before that I used to be terrified of talking to other people. Back when I owed money to the bank and other creditors, my fear of interactions was so deep that I would completely avoid their calls. I was afraid because I couldn't fathom how to pay them back. When I actually built up the courage to call them, I was surprised to learn that the situation was not nearly as scary as I'd made it out to be in my own head. All I had to do was reach out and communicate. Don't create unnecessary stress by avoiding a situation—deal with it proactively, having faith that things will work out better if you speak up and ask for help.

Don't create unnecessary stress by avoiding a situation—deal with it proactively, having faith that things will work out better if you speak up and ask for help.

4. **What core values do you aspire to live by?** Aside from the values already mentioned, I have five personal core values that make up the foundation of who I am.

- *Integrity*: Without integrity, nothing works. When things are out of balance in my life, I pause and consider the areas in which I might be out of integrity. I repeat this process on a daily basis until the problem is fixed. It's not comfortable, it's not selective, and it's never mastered—but it works.

- *Humility*: It's about being low profile and high impact. More people will be interested in you and your story when you're not boastful.

- *Gratitude*: My days start and end with this value. Practicing gratitude is a daily discipline that can completely alter a person's mindset. Gratitude helps me find balance between the pleasure and the pain that comes as a result of achieving a goal. Most people want to achieve something, but many often choose the path of least resistance and instant gratification. It's better to accept both the challenge and the reward equally as part of the journey. When you meet someone successful, it's pretty easy to tell whether they've endured challenges, failures, and adversity or whether their growth is fake. It comes across in their language, the tonality of their voice, and their body language. More importantly, it shows through their gratitude.

- *Love*: This is the ultimate act of acceptance. Whitney Houston said it best—"Learning to love yourself is the greatest love of all."
- *Appreciation*: What gets rewarded, gets repeated. I've found that lots of people will work harder for acknowledgment and recognition than they will for a paycheck. Employees often stick with low-paying jobs so long as their work is recognized because appreciation builds belief and confidence.

I read this list of core values every day because I want to become a person who embodies them as best I can.

It's better to accept both the challenge and the reward equally as part of the journey.

5. **Why do you do what you do? What gives your life meaning and purpose?** I find an abundance of joy and fulfillment in expanding people's mindsets or visions. Training and helping others become better at business has given my life purpose. Years ago, I was taught that *the secret to living is giving*. I've had the opportunity to influence many people throughout my life. I've been privileged to have had conversations with people in passing and on an airplane, helping some advance financially and sending others to seminars to improve their relationships. I've also successfully recommended deserving individuals for a promotion and facilitated introductions to create more business. I do these things because I find great joy and fulfillment in helping others level up. I find tremendous satisfaction in hearing the success stories of people who grow and expand through the opportunities I've had a hand in. Luck is when

preparation meets opportunity. If you want the rewards, you have to pay full price and you have to pay for it in advance. I have done both, so I feel like the luckiest guy in the world every day.

6. **How do you keep yourself physically healthy?** You can have all the success and money in the world, but without your health, you have nothing. Your health is your biggest asset—worth everything. *Your health is your wealth.* You have to find what works for you—what you can stay consistent with and commit to. For me, it's a combination of technology, community, nutrition, and activity. Hiking is definitely my go-to form of exercise, and I average over a hundred kilometers, or sixty miles, per week. I also love using my rebounder for high-intensity cardio, yet my apple watch is what really keeps me motivated to stay in shape. I'm in constant competition with myself to beat the little screen on my wrist. The way I see it, by the time the end of the day rolls around,

Training and helping others become better at business has given my life purpose.

either I'm going to beat the watch, or the watch is going to beat me. Somebody is going to win, and seldom do I lose. On the rare occasions when I don't win, I motivate myself to go out and do whatever it takes to meet the desired target for the day. After all, if you can't measure it, you can't track it. If you gather the right data, you'll know the right decisions to make moving forward.

I'm able to stay inspired from within by creating and gamifying competitions with myself as well as using technology to measure results. Lately my focus has been on increasing caloric expenditure each week. I've also found that a support team is an important component in achieving success in this area. Whether you recruit an expert smoothie maker or simply ask a friend for comradery and emotional support, I encourage everyone to seek out a support team. Who would have thought that me—the kid who was overlooked in gym class and ridiculed for not being athletic—is now the man at the front of the line every week in advanced hiking excursions? This fitness journey has changed my mindset to excel at an area in which I never have before. I am now taking my health very seriously; I'm also taking care of my teeth and eyes for the first time.

7. **How do you build your skill set?** Many years ago, I made a commitment to myself that I would read at least ten pages a day. Some days I read more, but I think ten pages is a very achievable number most of the time. It's easy to do, but it's also easy not to do. I've built up my skill set by making this a daily habit. This ten-page commitment leads to 3,650 pages a year, which is equivalent to reading twelve to fifteen books. Over time this powerful habit can compound and lead to massive results. Imagine reading the top bestselling books pertaining to a specific industry for three years. You'd gain a massive competitive edge and would likely dominate the field. This is how small habits and daily routines can lead to competitive strategies. I also listen to audiobooks while driving, sitting on planes, or during much of my downtime. The average person, in a major city, commutes about 500 hours per year. This equals to approximately a year of university education. Consider turning your car, bus, or train ride into a mobile university.

I've also found it necessary to find mentors, to be a part of mastermind groups, and to discover other forms of collective intelligence. Autobiographies and educational videos, particularly those on success and growth, help me stay sharp. Also, every Friday, I focus my energies on all topics relating to building wealth. Wealth day is structured into my calendar because I believe in dedicating time to the things you want in life. I also believe that it's necessary to be a part of a tribe of like-minded people. If you're the dumbest person in a group of people, then you've got the most to learn. This is the biggest gift of all, so don't be shy to ask for help or advice. Then, when you're in a place to do so, be sure to give back. Seek to restore the value proposition equilibrium so that everyone wins. Overall, it's about constantly pushing yourself beyond your comfort zone and never giving yourself permission to remain complacent. You're either growing or you're dying.

8. **How have you developed your cultural intelligence and your ability to get along with people who are very different from you?** Experiencing the world firsthand through travel has given me a more complete understanding of the infinite ways people choose to live. When I travel, I often veer off the beaten path—I've learned that doing so leads to more authentic, real experiences. Living locally, even for just a few days, has taught me more about different cultures and countries than any other form of learning. My relationship with Tatiana has also shaped my view of the world and all the people in it. She's helped fill in many of the gaps in my cultural awareness that I had had for most of my life. I also do my best to listen to a variety of music from all over the globe.

9. **How have you picked yourself up in times of adversity? What gives you the resilience to get through?** To reiterate, habits and routines give me the strength to push through the lows in life. If you abide by non-negotiable habits and routines, then peaks and valleys have less power over your emotions. I also think it's incredibly important to have gratitude. Investing your energy into negativity and complaints simply makes it that much harder for you to channel positive energy. An appreciative mindset works like a magnet, drawing in more of the good this world has to offer. I've also discovered ways to rekindle my energy in times of adversity. When I'm not feeling like myself, I wander into the woods and sit by the water for a while. This peaceful setting provides me with time to think and a space for creativity and reflection. I always leave in a much better mood, with new answers and perspectives and a greater passion for whatever it is I'm doing.

   That being said, there are times when all these practices combined are simply not enough to pull me out of a low in life. In these situations, I turn to others for help. I go to the people who strive for similar results, who share my understanding of integrity, and who live with heart centeredness—I turn to my tribe. Seek out those who think the way you do. Ideally this life team will support you the best; will help you out of a low; will be generous with their time, talents, and treasures; and will ensure that your mindset is one of abundance.

10. **What do you do to improve your brand and reputation?**
Relationship equity is a cornerstone in my approach to business and personal life. I do my best to keep others in mind as much as possible to create opportunities for greater relationships—both in terms of quantity and quality. My day-to-day reality involves expanding network connections via constant interaction on social media or in person. I go out of my way to appreciate people by calling, writing, and reaching out to people from so far in my past that most wouldn't even bother reconnecting. Tatiana and I famously phone our friends, family, and loved ones each year to sing them an off-tune birthday song ending with, "We hope you live to be a hundred, many years from now!" For several of these people, our call is one of the few things they have to look forward to on their birthday. I improve my brand and reputation by making myself memorable and making a difference in the lives of others.

I go to the people who strive for similar results, who share my understanding of integrity, and who live with heart centeredness—I turn to my tribe.

11. **How do you envision your ideal legacy?** I would like my legacy to be less about me and more about the meaningful, positive impact I've had on the world. I think problem solving is my planetary assignment. As I get older, I'm also seeing the value in developing timeless solutions to problems. My plan is to stay curious about life and continue searching for ways to influence new generations of people.

12. **Are you a part of a high-performing team?** I surround myself with a group of high-performing team members who together help keep my world in order. I've got a team of financial gurus, bookkeepers, and accountants as well as ultra-high net worth

individuals who endow me with advice on business and life. Together, this group of people essentially forms what Tony Jeary likes to call a life team. In his book *RESULTS, Faster!* Tony explains that life team members help you extend your ability to get things done, make better decisions, and do more of what you love. We all need support throughout our lives, so I encourage everyone to seek out the right people who will look out for you in the right ways.

13. **Do you have a favorite book? Why does it speak to you**? Dr. Stephen Covey's book *Seven Habits of Highly Effective People* has been one of the most influential books of my life. These core habits taught me how to live and work so that I could have an extraordinary quality of life. Dr. Covey was one of the first people in my life to definitively cause a paradigm shift that truly changed the way my mind works. It wasn't until later—when I was in Benin, West

My plan is to stay curious about life and continue searching for ways to influence new generations of people.

Africa—that I experienced a concept from this book in real time. I was a riding passenger in a car, when one of the tires suddenly went flat. Without hesitation, the driver hopped out of the car and started cutting grass from a nearby field. He then fixed the tire by stuffing it with the clippings, and we continued on our way. What I found to be an exceptional act of innovation was, for him, a simple solution based on common logic. Watching this driver's everyday fix forever changed my mindset. I have Dr. Covey to thank for bringing my awareness to our human tendency to carry around underlying assumptions and helping me experience what it feels like to break free from them.

14. **What is your two-minute, top tip of practical advice that others would find really useful?** Make a habit of asking yourself

the following two questions: (1) Where am I not requesting in my life? (2) Who do I become if I don't make requests? Like I said before, everything you want in life comes from your external world. Here is my biggest piece of advice—have the awareness to know when it's time to make a request, the courage to ask, and the wisdom to know what to ask for.

I hope that you can take the things that you have read in this book and apply them to create ripples of impact in your world and the world around you. I'm looking forward to hearing stories of how this book has influenced people's lives and the lives of others with whom they've shared it.

Dream big!

"Intentionally surround yourself with like-minded people who push you out of your comfort zone."

At the Board of Advisors Mastermind in Sarasota, Florida

"When the student is ready, the teacher appears."

eXp ringing the closing bell at NASDAQ for the first time.

The true purpose of goals is to compel you to become the person it takes to achieve them.

—Jim Rohn

APPENDIX

Introduction

VIPs

- ✔ The secret to living is giving. Enrich your life by putting the needs of others before your own. (Chapter 1)

- ✔ Having the mindset of an innovator can help you recognize opportunities to solve countless problems, which can in turn translate to a bigger bank account. (Chapter 2)

- ✔ Seek mentors, training, and development opportunities to help you discover your blind spots. (Chapter 3)

- ✔ Learn to embrace the present moment and celebrate the simple things in life. (Chapter 4)

- ✔ If you want real relationships that enrich your life, you must be real with others and especially with yourself. (Chapter 5)

- ✔ It's tough to be transparent with others when you are not in tune with yourself. The more you understand yourself, the better you're able to help other people understand themselves and the world around them. (Chapter 6)

- ✔ When you have the right mindset, collaboration becomes a powerful problem-solving tool. (Chapter 7)

- ✔ Tenacity is fundamental to every success story—past, present, and future. (Chapter 8)

CHAPTER 1 SERVICE

VIPs

✔ The secret to living is giving. Enrich your life by putting the needs of others before your own.

✔ Some of the best acts of service can be entirely spontaneous, so be on the lookout for opportunities to give.

✔ Be a go-giver, not a go-getter.

✔ To give without expectation is the greatest symbol of wealth.

CHAPTER 2 INNOVATION

VIPs

✔ We have the power to choose in which direction our childhood experiences propel us.

✔ Money is out there, it's just a matter of finding a way to turn obstacles into cash flow.

✔ Having the mindset of an innovator can help you recognize opportunities to solve countless problems, which can in turn translate to a bigger bank account.

✔ If you're feeling stuck in life, consider placing yourself in an *opportunity zone*—a place where you're surrounded by people who are more likely to benefit from your services.

✔ If you wish to be in close proximity to money that has already been made, then focus your energy on innovating connections and relationships. Once in this position, you can then leverage opportunities to grow and scale far more quickly than if you had simply focused your energy on making money alone. Work smarter, not harder.

CHAPTER 3 ABUNDANCE

VIPs

✔ Remember, no one is coming to rescue you.

✔ In life, you are either coming from a problem, in a problem, or heading toward a problem.

✔ BE, DO, and then HAVE.

✔ Your environment is always stronger than your willpower. Hence the importance of choosing the right environment.

✔ Seek mentors, training, and development opportunities to help you discover your blind spots.

CHAPTER 4 FUN

VIPs

✔ Don't just wait for fun to happen, schedule fun into your life and make it happen.

✔ Create a live list to do things now, instead of a bucket list planned for the end of your life.

✔ Learn to embrace the present moment and celebrate the simple things in life.

✔ Remember to always tell your face to smile.

✔ Speed is calculated by miles per hour, but *life* is calculated as smiles per hour. If you want extra mileage in life, simply smile more.

CHAPTER 5 RELATIONSHIPS

VIPs

✔ If you want real relationships that enrich your life, you must be real with others and especially with yourself.

✔ Seek to understand first and second to be understood.

✔ Learning to be unattached to the outcome allows you to make room for possibility.

✔ In most cases, your net worth mirrors the levels of your five closest friends. Who you spend your time with is who you become.

✔ It's up to you to protect your own energy and vision by being selective about who you choose to let into your inner circle.

CHAPTER 6 TRANSPARENCY

VIPs

✔ It's tough to be transparent with others when you are not in tune with yourself. The more you understand yourself, the better you're able to help other people understand themselves and the world around them.

✔ Be transparent about your shortcomings so that you may grow from them.

✔ When you're a nobody in a sea of accomplished people, it's easy to hide behind others. Reaching higher levels begets greater visibility and exposure.

✔ None of us are perfect, so there's no point in pretending to be.

CHAPTER 7   COLLABORATION

VIPs

✔ The world is a giant network of conversations; all you have to do is step into it.

✔ There is often an element of service to practicing collaboration. Working with someone, or a larger group of people, to achieve a common goal typically means giving up a piece of yourself to make things happen.

✔ When you have the right mindset, collaboration becomes a powerful problem-solving tool.

✔ If you happen to be a leader of a team or company, be sure to step outside of the office and connect with as many people in your organization as possible.

✔ Talking to the voice inside your head for too long can lead to *analysis paralysis*. Get out of your head and connect with others to make the most of life.

CHAPTER 8 TENACITY

VIPs

✔ Tenacity is fundamental to every success story—past, present, and future.

✔ I make decisions based on whether a result will bring me more freedom or less freedom.

✔ My life changed when I stopped making announcements, started taking action, and began earning experience through hard work.

✔ It's about using your assets to pay for your lifestyle—not just your money.

✔ Tenacity alone holds little value. Tenacity combined with a clear direction and a strong ability to focus leads to wins.

✔ Life isn't happening to you; it's happening for you.

Leaders Yielding 2 New Knowledge, LY2NK Foundation, is my family foundation for global philanthropy projects. Our goal is to transform the human spirit by empowering people through education, mentorship, and the transfer of knowledge. We are currently establishing the first LY2NK Leadership Academy in Liberia, West Africa. If you'd like to learn more about the ripple of impact we are creating through education, or you want to be a part of empowering others, please join us at www.LY2NK.org.

Follow us on our journey at Facebook,
Instagram, and LinkedIn.

LY2NK Foundation
My Family Foundation for Global Philanthropy Projects
www.Ly2nk.org

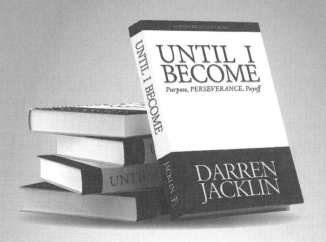

Thank you for reading my book!

I hope that throughout the journey, you've gained insight
that has led you to new ideas, solutions, and mindsets.
If that's the case, please share your story with our
team by contacting us at **tatiana@darrenjacklin.com**,
or, if you'd like to place a bulk order for copies
of this book to share, gift, or donate, please call
604.803.9622. We look forward to hearing from you!

www.darrenjacklin.com
www.untilibecome.com